CROSS-TRAINING:
The Complete Book of the Triathlon

CROSS-TRAINING:
The Complete Book of the Triathlon

KATHERINE VAZ
and the Editors of Triathlon magazine

 AVON
PUBLISHERS OF BARD, CAMELOT, DISCUS AND FLARE BOOKS

AVON BOOKS
A division of
The Hearst Corporation
1790 Broadway
New York, New York 10019

for Neil Feineman

Acknowledgments

First thanks go to my parents, August and Elizabeth Vaz, and to my brothers and sisters—Mark, Maria, Patrick, Peter, and Teresa—for their love and support.

Thereafter a note of gratitude to *Triathlon* magazine, particularly Michael Gilmore, Penny Little, and Harald Johnson, who were the first magazine publishers on the block to light upon the cross-training trend. Special thanks to Harald Johnson for his help on this book's photography. How far could I have gone without the rest of the *Triathlon* crew? Patti Benner, Stephanie Chiacos, Nancy Mock, and Daemon Filson encouraged me every step of the way.

John Jerome, who writes a monthly column in *Outside* magazine, was particularly generous with his past interviews with David Costill. Jeanette Foster, the 1983 Ironman press coordinator, gave me free access to the statistics and interviews she has compiled. Barclay Kruse gave me technical assistance in the cycling chapter and Jeff Galloway in running. Bob Anderson, author of *Stretching*, designed a program for triathletes specifically for this book (a fold-out chart is available, 22½ inches by 33 inches, $4.00 postpaid from Stretching, Inc., P.O. Box 767, Palmer Lake, CO 80133), and Ellen Coleman, author of *Eating for Endurance*, (available for $6.00 postpaid, 5336 Bardwell, Riverside, CA 92506), was unsparing in her help toward developing Chapter 8.

Final thanks to Meg Pokrass, Annie Brody, Neil Feineman, Alan Rodin, and my editor Bill Alexander, all instrumental in getting this project off the ground. My hat, if I'd ever get around to wearing one, is off to those ambitious athletes and pioneer exercise physiologists, dozens of whom consented to be interviewed, who have made cross-training into the premier exercise frontier. They are sleeker and swifter than I, and I couldn't have done it without them.

Contents

CROSS-TRAINING:
The Complete Book of the Triathlon

On Being Strangers at the Party

A *note from the author*

My swimming instructor, his nose plastered with white zinc oxide, brandished a Red Cross report card at me. My friends and assorted other 10-year-olds reclined on soggy beach towels at the Castro Valley Pool (an easy drive from Oakland, California), unwrapping licorice vines to celebrate the end of our August session and the awarding of diplomas. It seemed a peaceful enough interlude in a child's summer wasteland.

Even the simplest day of reckoning is not without its terrible swift sword, however. I hadn't aced much beyond dolphin dives, but I hardly suspected that my flailing had driven Rob of the clown nose to such frenzy that he felt no recourse but to emblazon "WEAK!!" in stark, indelible red across my entire card.

My friends wanted to see my grades. Wouldn't intermediate swimming next summer be a blast? Had I received a "good," "fair," or "needs work" on my breaststroke? They tore the report card from my hands, and after the first humiliation, as they say, there is no other.

After a moment of silence, one of my friends hissed, "So what. He's the one with that stupid nose." Even on that distant afternoon I sensed that in the hierarchy of trauma this vignette would have to be awarded quite a low rank, and what mattered was always to have loyal and outspoken allies. Nevertheless it would be almost 15 years before I climbed back into the water.

That's when Betty Talbot came along to change my sports reticence. One morning, with the Santa Ana winds blowing hot off the desert to unsettle an already sweltering Los Angeles, she and I arrived simultaneously at the downtown office of *Swim Swim* to turn in copy. We both worked for the magazine as freelancers, and this was the first time we'd run into each other.

Betty, in her mid-50s, wore a big shell necklace and smiled brightly. I was half her age, but she set such a blistering pace climbing the four flights of stairs to the office that trying to catch up with her gave me one of those rare moments of flash revelation. Every lunchtime for the past 10 years, summer and winter, Betty had been marching alone through the breakers of the Pacific and swimming a mile. Her vibrancy was a simple but graphic lesson in cause and effect. Suddenly my options became quite clear. I could learn from her independent spirit, or I could continue laboring under the misconception that being small and thin was insurance against turning phlegmatic by the time I was 40.

The next morning I struggled through a few hundred yards at the YMCA pool in West Los Angeles. One year later I could swim a mile in about 30 minutes. (World-record performers, to give you an idea of relative speeds, can race that distance in half the time.) I wasn't burning up the lanes, but I was consistent enough to ease onto the low rung of structured classes that emphasized interval training. Now, on days when I either need a change of scene or know I can't get to the pool, I'll put in a running workout before breakfast.

I mention all this not as a haphazard character study, but because it's important to establish who I am—a 28-year-old native Californian, but hardly a golden girl—and how I have come to write about cross-training and triathloning, a sport usually described as "grueling," "punishing," and "obsessive."

I was asked to write *Cross-Training: The Complete Book of the Triathlon* because for the past few years I've had one of the best seats in the house to watch triathloning excite and confound the sports world. Triathloning, to dispense with the technical definition at the outset, is a system of training that incorporates three sports, usually swimming, cycling, and running, or a race in which the three segments are completed consecutively. By the end of the 1983 season, about 250,000 participants entered over 1000 triathlons internationally, with 600,000 predicted to enter over 1800 races in 1984. We've been watching a fitness idea germinate into a sensibility—and a big business—right before our eyes.

My front-and-center seat has been courtesy of Michael Gilmore, Harald Johnson, and Penny Little, who decided to publish *Swim Swim* about six years ago. In Los Angeles, given the short life expectancy of independent productions, that's practically a declaration of war. They always delivered clean, high-quality work, which I took as a sign that something exciting was in the cards.

That turned out to be *Triathlon* magazine, the result of a one-time test-market special called *Swim-Bike-Run*, produced soon after I joined them as their senior editor. We expected a good response and instead were overwhelmed. Renaissance athletics, meaning an emphasis on versatility and endurance instead of on sheer strength and speed, was apparently resurgent. We took our lead from this groundswell and published the premier issue of *Triathlon* in spring 1983.

Our greatest publicity boost came from the Bud Light Hawaiian Ironman Triathlon World Championship, a 2.4-mile ocean swim immediately followed by a 112-mile bike ride and a full 26.2-mile run—a race of such daring that it has staggered everyone's imagination, not to mention a number of entrants, since its debut in 1978. Given our penchant for superlatives—the longest day, the fastest man alive—reporters knew a monumental story when they saw it. Here was the greatest mass-participation endurance contest ever devised.

It quickly spawned hundreds of shorter-distance triathlons around the world. Magazines, newspapers, videotapes, and television hurled multisport events into the limelight, but the Ironman's intimidating proportions may have obscured the underlying principles described in Chapter 1 that paradoxically make triathloning more forgiving and accessible than most other sports.

For one thing, about 90 percent of all triathlons are considerably scaled down from the Ironman. Last year, for example, nearly

1000 women entered the Bonne Bell Triathlon: 1K swim, 30K bike, 10K run (in rounded-off miles, that's about ½, 20, 6), held at Marine World/Africa U.S.A., a theme park near San Francisco. A race of these more typical dimensions is to the Ironman what your local 10K footrace is to the Boston Marathon.

For high-powered performers, multisport events are the perfect "beyond-a-marathon" frontier, the ultimate aerobic test. For people like me, the variety found in cross-training keeps fitness a living process that's less likely to slip into automatic pilot. It also means better overall conditioning and total body fitness. To put it another way, unless you're an Olympic contender or a professional athlete who specializes in one sport, why settle for swimmer's shoulders or cyclist's legs when you can have both?

Now I come to the other reason I was asked to write this book. If I can distill useful concepts from the enormity of the Ironman—ideas that have radically changed my outlook on health and fitness—so can you. You'll even discover ways to apply cross-training principles to other avenues of your life.

If you have often felt like the stranger at the party in athletic matters but hold to the tenets of a strong mind in a strong body, cross-training and its direct application through triathlon competitions will do nothing short of changing everything you've ever believed about fitness.

In the first section of this book, I explain the principles of cross-training and the history of multisport events. Many exercise physiologists and doctors insist that the classic definition of "cross-training" refers only to physiological effects, not to a system of training. They prefer calling the whole system "expanded training" or "multisport training," and I use their terms when quoting them or mentioning their work. Most triathletes, however, use "cross-training" to describe the method of exercise whereby practicing one sport increases one's power and agility in another sport, and therefore it is my main term throughout.

The second section explores swimming, cycling, running, and the art of making transitions for novice triathletes. Each of the three sports easily warrants its own book, of course, and I list a number of good references at the end of these chapters to provide more detailed technical information than space allows

Betty Talbot, 58, gets set for the 1984 Penguin Swim—a 500-yard, 60-degree plunge on New Year's Day. She won the Queen's crown in 1975.

HARALD JOHNSON

here. In the text I concentrate on ways that novices can apply the concepts explained in the first section to each of the disciplines.

Finally, the last part of the book—an invitation to the party for beginners—tells you exactly what to expect in a triathlon and how to get involved. If you have no intention of ever competing, the sections on mental preparation, nutrition, and goal setting will still give direction to your training. If you are already involved in a fitness program and think a race would be perfect for gauging your "personal best" times, this section will help you get to the starting line of a short-distance triathlon within about one year, *given the same amount of time you're now spending to train in one sport.*

One final note: When writing about a new and largely untested subject, one always runs the risk of wishing a few years later that all the current information could be magically penciled into the margins of the published work. If linking three sports together is the current rage, why shouldn't four be far behind? What tangible data will we have from David Costill's Human Performance Laboratory and from the host of scientists now investigating fitness? Various organizations are vying for control of the sport, and new stars emerge monthly.

Right now we're on the cutting edge of triathloning. If nothing else, the excitement that results is what I aim to convey. Given enough time, everything invites revisionism; everything changes. For instance, I no longer see white zinc oxide, my old nemesis, at the beach. And as for Betty Talbot, the last I heard she planned to take her time designing and building a house for herself in Kona, Hawaii. The moral of the story is that the scenery often changes, but impulses of vitality never waver.

Los Angeles
November 1983

PART 1

A Cross-Training Primer

Why an inordinate amount of interest in animals and athletes? They are subjects for art and exemplars of it, are they not?

—Marianne Moore (1887–1972)
A Marianne Moore Reader (1961)

When I turned 40 I suddenly realized how many things scared me. For instance, I was afraid to put my face in a lake or in any open water. I took my fears as a sign of growing old.

I decided I was at a turning point and I'd better act fast. I practiced swimming with an inflatable inner tube, and about a year later I entered the Sri Chinmoy Triathlon. When the time came, I still couldn't put my face in. I swam backstroke the whole way. I didn't finish in the allotted time, which put me out of the race. But I finished the cycling and running anyway and then got right back in the water to finish what I'd missed.

There's something addictive about it. Triathlons are like having babies. During labor you think, "Oh my God, what a mistake!" But then when it's over, you think, "Well, that wasn't too bad!" That's why I keep entering triathlons—long after conquering my fear of putting my face in the water.

—Millie Brown, 44, Connecticut
Children's ice skating instructor
(and mother of three)

CHAPTER 1

Cross-Training: The new lease on your sports life

The wilds of Koshima, an island off the east coast of Japan, provided the setting years ago for a discovery so startling that it reigns as one of social science's most remarkable lessons. It all started when scientists studying the habits of a tribe of *Macaca fuscata* monkeys since the early 1920s fed their subjects by tossing sweet potatoes into the sand. The monkeys enjoyed the food but disliked the grit.

Then in the autumn of 1958, an 18-month-old female monkey named Imo (to give credit where credit is due) discovered that washing the potatoes in a nearby stream took the rough edges off the repast. She taught this culinary refinement to her mother. A number of Imo's peers learned the skill in turn and then demonstrated it to their mothers.

Soon scientists recorded an astounding breakthrough. Choosing a number for the sake of argument, suppose that on one morning 99 *Macaca fuscata* monkeys had finally figured out how to wash their breakfast. Suppose further that by noon the hundredth monkey had learned.

By nightfall, every monkey on the island was washing sweet potatoes before eating them. That hypothetical "hundredth monkey" somehow broke through all existing barriers, as if that final, measurable act of consent opened the ideological and physical doors for everyone.

The best is yet to come. No sooner had that hundredth monkey split wide open the social habits of the Koshima locals, when scientists observing other monkey colonies on outlying islands and on the mainland at Takasakiyama reported an amazing phenomenon. All those faraway monkeys, with no immediate example and certainly with no training, suddenly began unearthing their own caches of sweet potatoes from the sand and washing them. The complete lesson had jumped intact over the sea!

The *morphogenetic field theory* behind this hundredth-monkey phenomenon asserts that when only a limited number of people adopt a new way, it remains their exclusive territory. But there is a point at which if only one more person becomes attuned to that new awareness, a field is created whereby it is accessible to (although not necessarily implemented by) everyone everywhere.

Consider how aptly this applies to athletic arenas. Soviet gymnast Olga Korbut stunned her worldwide audience during the 1972 Munich Olympics when she firmly planted both her feet on the top of the uneven parallel bars and flipped backward. She whipped around through the air and grabbed the top bar cleanly. She also did this same back flip from a standing position on the balance beam. It didn't look just difficult—it looked impossible, utterly beyond the mechanical range of a human being.

The galvanizing effect of her superhuman maneuver and the emotional response of all who witnessed it carried her through the rest of her routines to an unprecedented number of perfect scores. It also bewitched thousands of prepubescent girls around the world into scurrying to the gym. Whatever chord of magic or prowess had been struck, it didn't take long before the hundredth-monkey phenomenon turned Korbut's incredible backward somersault into a standard move off the high bar, an integral component of every competition-caliber female gymnast's routine. It no longer elicits a gasp of disbelief from an audience. Nor does it seem a feat of breathless daring beyond the grasp of human ability.

These images emanating from the morphogenetic field theory

keep recurring when I consider that triathloning skills suddenly seem accessible to an increasing number of people. "Most of us learned how to swim, bike, and run as children," says Kathleen McCartney, 24, who won the February 1982 Ironman with no previous competitive background. "These are skills most of us have already."

Childhood skills, to be sure—but combined in ingenious new ways. The preceding monkey business illustrates that breaking through barriers sometimes comes via disarmingly simple acts.

To put it another way, legions have already risen to the challenge of running marathons. Since athletics thrives on breakthroughs, what's the new outer boundary? Triathlons are the biggest collective fitness invitation in years to push beyond what we think we can do and to surpass universally accepted limits on our energy. "It's important not to become part of your chair," warns 48-year-old triathlete Carol Hogan.

Break on through:
Raising the ceiling on human performance

Few have explored human physical potential with a greater or more professional sense of adventure than Dr. David Costill, director of the Human Performance Laboratory at Ball State University in Muncie, Indiana.

His pursuit of scientific truth once led him to swallow 12 ounces of corn oil to test how concentrated triglycerides affect the bloodstream. Memories of that punitive cocktail still make him wince. "I have trouble now even eating a fatty meal," he says.

Undaunted, he continues as his own best cross-training laboratory. "I was a sprint swimmer in college, a little better than mediocre," says the 48-year-old Costill. "Then about 15 years ago I started running, and I couldn't believe I would ever run a mile. Now I've done a few marathons. The body's capacity for improving itself in response to physical stress amazes me. I don't have the physiology to run a great marathon, but through properly managed stress I can transcend my own athletic history." With that philosophy in mind, Costill's recent return to swimming merited him a national championship in the 45–49 age group for the 50-meter freestyle and 2-mile swim.

Instead of following Costill's example of focusing within ourselves to discover individual potential, most of us resort to
athletic mimicry. We work from the outside in by watching world-
class runners dash down the road, and then imitating how they
train and the length of their strides. David Costill and other sports
scientists around the world are trying to understand exactly *how*
and *why* the fastest runners are fast. We can then apply the data
to our own physiologies. "You're out to achieve your highest
potential, not change your anatomy," says Costill.

Take one illustrative case. Muscle biopsies, one of Costill's best-
known areas of study, indicate a person's ratio of slow-twitch to
fast-twitch muscle fibers. Sports scientists have discovered that a
person with a higher percentage of fast-twitch fibers will perform
better in sprint events, while more slow-twitch fibers indicate a
greater aptitude for long distances. Since we are born with a
certain ratio, this study gives us concrete evidence that genetics
plays an important role in our athletic potential.

Costill's lab, incidentally, advocates biopsies only for research.
"You can't physiologically change slow-twitch fibers to fast," says
Costill. "I don't think there's any reason to psychologically under-
mine someone who's trying to be faster by announcing what
might be construed as a discouraging percentage."

Because discoveries always goad further explorations, new
methods of obtaining biopsies in turn prompted studies on how
the muscles are affected by prolonged endurance exercise, of
which triathloning is one example. How much are our physical
limitations determined by the efficient conveyance of oxygen to
the muscles, and how much by the ability of those muscles to use
the oxygen they receive?

In other words, what combination of cardiovascular training
and muscular development yields the best results? What combination of sports, and at what intensity, will lead an athlete to
optimum conditioning? Because work at the cellular level on this
subject is a new frontier, exercise physiologists admit that so far
no one has any final answers.

"We're already aware that exercise improves the quality of life,"
says John Duncan at the Cooper Clinic in Dallas. (Dr. Kenneth
Cooper is considered one of the founding fathers of the aerobic
movement.) "We know that exercise *probably* improves blood

David Costill's studies at the Human Performance Laboratory have expanded our understanding about athletic endurance.

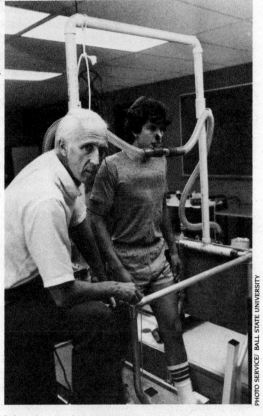

PHOTO SERVICE/ BALL STATE UNIVERSITY

clotting, cholesterol levels, and metabolic, psychological, and hormonal problems. Right now we're trying to come up with concrete proof."

"What we do know," sums up John Kovaleski, who works in Costill's lab, "is that science can eventually get us back in touch with what the body is capable of doing."

For now, though, the body's capabilities are largely inexplicable. Notice that the record for the mile set by Walter Slade in 1875 was 4:25.5. Nine years later, Walter George could manage to run an impressive 6.1 seconds faster. Roger Bannister finally broke the 4-minute barrier almost 80 years later (see the "Milestones" chart).

After Bannister, record breaking in the mile slowed dramatically.

Runners shaved off only fractions of seconds. "Once a certain level is reached, it's harder to improve," says Kovaleski.

A perfect example is Filbert Bayi's 3:51.0 in 1975, which broke Jim Ryun's 8-year record of 3:51.1 by the most infinitesimal of margins. Finally, in 1981 Sebastian Coe of Great Britain delivered a 3:47.3, the world record as of 1983. The higher the standard, the more hairsplitting the process of excellence.

I remember a top California ocean swimmer, desperately searching for a way to encourage me after watching my stroke,

In 1875 Walter Slade's 4:24.5-minute mile received accolades, but to-day it would hardly attract notice. Notice how the record breaking moves by leaps and bounds up to the 4-minute mark and slows there-after. Once a new record is set, the critical mass seems automatically

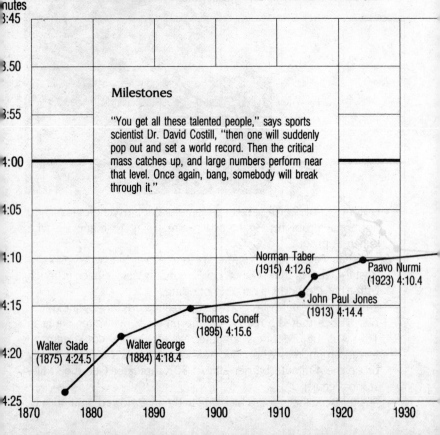

Milestones

"You get all these talented people," says sports scientist Dr. David Costill, "then one will suddenly pop out and set a world record. Then the critical mass catches up, and large numbers perform near that level. Once again, bang, somebody will break through it."

Walter Slade (1875) 4:24.5
Walter George (1884) 4:18.4
Thomas Coneff (1895) 4:15.6
John Paul Jones (1913) 4:14.4
Norman Taber (1915) 4:12.6
Paavo Nurmi (1923) 4:10.4

saying, "You're going to have the excitement of being able to knock *whole minutes* off your time. The rest of us are stuck battling with split seconds." A roundabout compliment if ever I heard one, but it's true that in the early stages of a pursuit we progress by leaps and bounds. Triathloning is so untested that most of us can look forward to the reward of slicing minutes, not seconds, off our time.

The early years of the Hawaiian Ironman (2.4-mile swim, 112-mile bike, 26.2-mile run) have clearly followed this same pattern.

"drawn up" to higher levels of performance. Although scientists suggest that the 3:30 mile may be the ultimate time barrier, they also admit that the astounding (remember Bob Beamon's long jump in the 1968 Mexico City Olympics?) should never be ruled out.

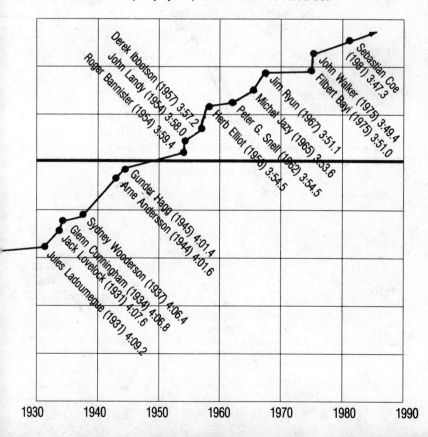

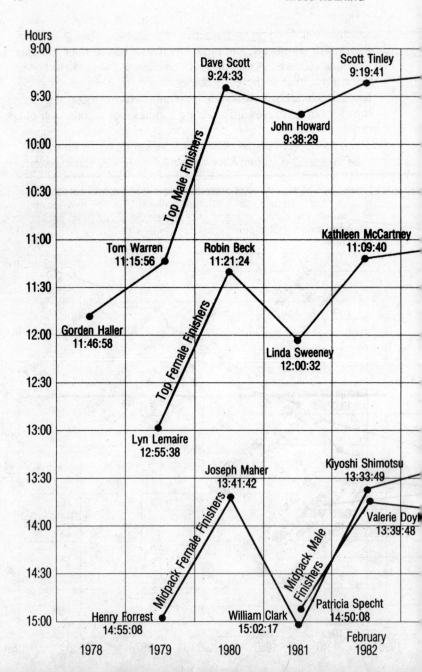

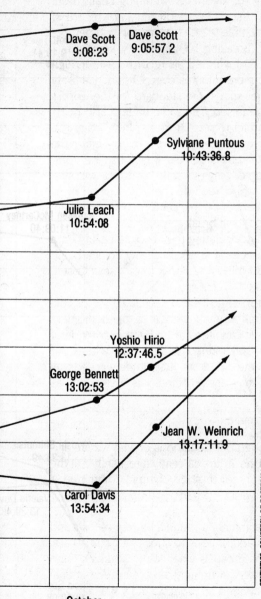

Dave Scott
9:08:23

Dave Scott
9:05:57.2

Sylviane Puntous
10:43:36.8

Julie Leach
10:54:08

Yoshio Hirio
12:37:46.5

George Bennett
13:02:53

Jean W. Weinrich
13:17:11.9

Carol Davis
13:54:34

October
1982

1983

STATISTICS: COURTESY OF FOSTER/GAFFNEY ASSOCIATES, HAWAII

Stories of Iron

Note that the dramatic jump made by both the top male and female finishers in 1980 *was also made by Joseph Maher*, who finished directly in midpack that year. Although 1981 proved a tougher year for all competitors, the ensuing races show a continual upgrade. What's compelling here is to observe how the times of the midpack finishers—in all cases the ones who ended up exactly halfway through the computer list—rise and fall in exact accordance with the winners.

The female midpack finisher data is inconclusive, since no women ran in 1978, only one woman competed in 1979, and in 1980 the second of only two female entrants finished near the end.

In 1980, Dave Scott, then 26, a former swimming coach from Davis, California, knocked almost *2 hours* off the 1979 record of 11:15:56 by posting an incredible 9:24:33. Many top competitors immediately began to see "breaking 10" as the new standard.

By 1983, however, Scott had whittled his record down enough to break the winner's tape mere minutes over 9 hours. It's likely that when the 9-hour barrier snaps, the standard for the world's best triathletes will again be raised. The same pattern also holds true for the top women triathletes (see "Stories of Iron," page 16).

These statistics return us rather neatly to what happened on the island of Koshima. Bold strokes render old ways obsolete. "You get all these talented people," says Costill, "and one will suddenly pop out and set a world record. Then the critical mass catches up, and large numbers of people perform near that level. Once again, bang, somebody will break through it."

Is there a way of precisely calculating the absolute ceiling on a certain skill? "It seems inconceivable now that any human being could possibly break a 3:30 mile, but who knows?" says Costill. "Anything might be possible."

We've all heard those stories—if it's the seemingly impossible you're after—about the frail woman who in a blind moment of adrenalin-producing panic can lift a car up by its rear fender if she sees her husband or son pinned underneath. Where our power springs from, and the times its magnitude exceeds all discernible physical laws, may always remain as mysterious as acts of creativity.

The will to endure

Other evidence has expanded our definitions of who we are and what we can accomplish. John Troup, currently a researcher at the Sports Physiology Laboratory for the U.S. Olympic Committee in Colorado Springs, worked with Costill in 1979 on a study about age and endurance.

"We ran some Masters swimmers through a battery of tests and discovered that the body's adaptations to stress past age 40 are, as you might guess, not as great as when we're younger," says Troup. (Information on Masters swimming, an organized national program for adults, is provided in Chapter 4.) "But we also discovered that up until age 50, the maximum aerobic capacity decreases *at a lower rate* than other components of a person's fitness, such as strength."

This slower decrease in endurance capacity means that athletes who have developed a solid level of aerobic conditioning over the years *can perform at a higher level in endurance events for more years than they can in events emphasizing other skills such as strength, dexterity, or sprinting.* "It's good news for expanded training and for older people," says Troup.

By way of example, *40 percent* of the October 1982 Ironman participants were 30 to 39 years old. It isn't unusual for an over-30 Masters swimmer to discover that after years of continued training, he's doing his best times since college. The kids will still run past you, but despite the inevitable performance declines that come with growing older, there's no documentable reason to figure that all your moments of athletic pride are behind you. See "Ultraendurance Races," next page.

All evidence suggests that endurance events such as triathlons are made to order for average people who develop above-average aerobic capacities. "The pacing and intensity required in this sport take a long time to develop. You have to be mature to do well," says Jann Girard, 21, an up-and-coming triathlete and college student from Austin, Texas. "That's what's exciting. I can look forward to getting better all the time."

"The older I get, the fitter I become," says triathlete Mary Ann Buxton, 41, a product manager for Levi's. "Or maybe it's that I can now see there aren't any barriers."

Ted Pulaski, 42, puts it even more graphically. "When I left law school I stopped working out for 20 years," he says. "I was a smoker and a drinker and obese. When I hit 40 I weighed 200 pounds. I was really a slob. I looked like death warmed over."

Then one day he watched ABC-TV cover the Ironman on "Wide World of Sports." "That was the challenge I wanted. I quit smoking, drinking, and gorging myself," says the former Marine parachute jumper. "My whole life-style became so different that eventually I had different friends. I found I had more in common with a 20-year-old triathlete than with a 42-year-old businessman who wanted to smoke cigarettes and play cards all night long."

Ultraendurance Races, 1983

At *least half* of the finishers in each of these 1983 races were 30 or older. In fact, the greater the number of participants, the higher the percentage, suggesting that the less esoteric the long-distance event,

Race	Approximate Distance (in Miles)	No. of Entrants
Second Annual Swim Around Manhattan (Swimming)	28.5	28
Race Across America (Cycling)	3150	12
New York City Marathon (Running)	26.2	15,193
Ironman World Championship (Swim, Bike, Run)	2.4 swim 112 bike 26.2 run	964

Such testimony proves that the current assessment of triathletes as obsessed has distracted us from the virtues of cross-training. Tennis instructors don't insist that you either learn to volley like Björn Borg or surrender your racquet. Why, then, this deluge of gnashing-of-teeth adjectives to describe triathlons? Dave Scott and other high-caliber performers are no more compulsive about their sport than Jack Nicklaus is about golf. Cross-training makes too much sense to leave for just the big kids.

Cross-education comes of age

The classic definition of cross-training is that when one muscle group is exercised, a corresponding muscle group also shows increased strength, *even if it is kept stationary,* as long as the motor nerves to the inactive part are uninjured. A leg kept immobile by a cast, for instance, will become stronger if the other leg is exercised.

Before the turn of the century, physiologists and psychologists demonstrated that training one limb resulted in significant imthe more inviting it becomes for mass participation by those over 30. In the New York City Marathon, for example, the 30–39 category had 952 women finishers and 5072 men finishers, making it by far the largest age group to enter the race.

No. of Finishers	No. of Finishers 30 and Over		Total Finishers Over 30	% of Finishers 30 and Over (Approx.)
	Men	Women		
21	6	5	11	52
6	3	0	3	50
14,546	9646	1475	11,121	76
835	463	58	521	62

STATISTICS: DRURY GALLAGHER, ROBERT HUSTWIT, JAMES GLUCKSON, JEANETTE FOSTER

provements in the symmetrical but *unexercised* limb. They called this *cross-education*, and it applied both to learning new skills and to improvement of strength. They noticed that overload training in the active limb, meaning work done at a high level of stress or intensity, was necessary to produce the same effect on the unexercised limb that that arm or leg would acquire through low-stress exercise on its own.

Why this works is still unclear. Some physiologists have deduced from their studies of the body's motor pathways from the cortex (the outer part of the brain) that 70 to 85 percent of our nerve fibers cross from one side of the body to the other in their descent through the spinal cord. This means that well over half our nerves branch into opposite sides of the body but receive impulses from a common source. Cross-education occurs when the stimulation is great enough from overload training to affect the nerves that cross over from the muscles in the active limb to the inactive muscle on the other side.

Researchers found during cross-education experiments that *isometric contractions (meaning identical muscular reactions) actually occurred in the inactive limbs* when the corresponding parts were exercising. Fatigued muscles could be kept working longer by having the dormant limb begin synchronous movement, not necessarily at an overload level. These discoveries of how the body's interdependent system can trade off the workload and reach maximum strength and efficiency have revolutionized physical therapy and sports medicine.

Thinking of your body in this way—as an interconnected mechanism instead of as an assemblage of independent parts—can help you understand cross-training in a larger sense. If you wish to improve the way you throw a baseball, for example, your first thought might be to improve and develop explosive power in your anterior deltoid, pectoralis major, triceps brachii, rotators of the forearm, and flexors in your wrist. These are the shoulder, chest, and arm muscles you will employ when pitching the ball.

But other muscles do come into play. When you throw the baseball, you twist your trunk, change the pressure on your feet, and balance the movement with your head and hips. Endurance must figure into the total picture as well. No one can afford to lose pitching strength halfway through a game. Building muscle mass for strength will help the velocity at which you throw the ball, but high-repetition, sustained-contraction exercises are what develop endurance. You must also condition your body to perform under stress. The final test is how well you function when tired.

Expanded training's broad focus is the best way to tackle the greatest number of these tangential considerations. Flexibility, strength, and cardiovascular work will each develop a separate component of what you might have dismissed as the relatively uncomplicated act of throwing a ball. "Balance and variety are the keys to overall fitness," says Mark Allen, two-time winner of the Nice Triathlon in France.

Many athletes now use this physiological model of cross-training to describe the pervasive benefits that transfer from one sport to another. "Training different muscle groups enables some of the fitness gained in one sport to cross over into another," explains Richard Marks, 35, a triathlete and marathon swimmer. Many triathletes credit Sally Edwards, a top-ranking competitor, with popularizing the term through her book *Triathlon: A Triple Fitness Sport*, the first manual on the subject.

Adopting more than one training system for better overall conditioning sounds like a straightforward concept, but most of us still think in terms of choosing "my sport"—one well-defined, amenable fitness niche. Many people dismiss expanded training on the presupposition that they have barely enough time for one sport, let alone several.

You needn't do all three sports every day, as top triathletes do. Part 2 explains how to include several disciplines in varying measure in your current time schedule. The following sections of this chapter detail how cross-training affects specific muscle groups.

The agonist and the ecstasy

Among the various muscle groups in your body are *agonist* muscles that shorten and thus initiate movement and *antagonists* that lengthen but oppose the movement. The agonists (from the Greek *agonistikos*, "fit for combat") are the prime movers, but the antagonists control the intensity of the motion. Agonists allow you to turn your head, for instance, but the corresponding antagonists keep you from imitating Linda Blair's head-spinning act in *The Exorcist*. Most sports injuries occur when the antagonists are not strong enough to keep the pull of the agonists in check. If all working and opposing muscles are strong, you are less likely to injure yourself.

In cycling, for example, your quadriceps (the tops of your thighs) contract while your hamstrings (the backs of your legs) relax. In running, the opposite happens; your hamstrings are the prime movers, and your quadriceps lengthen and oppose the exercise. The shin muscles are flexed during cycling, whereas the calf muscles on the opposite side get a superior workout from running.

By incorporating both cycling and running into your schedule (you needn't always do both during every workout), you're strengthening the agonists along with the antagonists—all the interlocking quadriceps, hamstring, shin, and calf muscles in your legs. Cross-training makes the entire intrastructure strong and thus less susceptible to pulls or spasms. It also promotes smoother interaction between connective muscle groups.

To give a comparable illustration in swimming, consider that as your arm stretches out, enters the water, and pulls you forward, you're flexing your pectorals and the anterior fibers of your deltoid muscles (the large, triangular muscles that enable you to lift your arms away from your sides).

When your arm then lifts out of the water during the recovery phase of your stroke, the trapezius and posterior fibers in those same deltoids are contracting as the pectorals and anterior fibers relax. This strengthens the agonist and antagonist muscle groups in your shoulder, chest, and back; your biceps and forearms, although necessary for powering through the water, receive less concentrated attention.

For that and other comparable reasons, many coaches now endorse strength training for fitness swimmers who hope to make the most out of often limited time available for the pool. Arm curls are specifically recommended to develop the biceps, thereby strengthening the entire cross-connected structure of arm muscles. Dry-land work zeros in on the muscles that come into secondary play and develops explosive power in the applicable interlocking structures in less time than it would take for swimming to reach them.

Sports specificity

Before describing in detail the ways cross-training can help you, it's important to explain the ways in which it won't. Elite performers, especially in sprint events or races under 2 hours, won't necessarily turn in faster times in their sport of choice by expanded training.

"It's hard to see how a cycling-time trialist would improve through running," says Stan Lindstedt, Ph.D., of the University of Wyoming at Laramie, echoing the sentiments of coaches who feel that elite athletes must use all their available time to concentrate on their specialty.

Sports specificity maintains that the only way to be a better swimmer, for example, is by swimming and focusing on those exercises that will directly develop the chosen sport. An isokinetic swim bench, which allows a simulated front-crawl motion on dry land, is one accessory for serious swimmers.

Lindstedt, to prove his case, performed muscle biopsies that showed a higher mitochondria density (a key determinant of a cell's energy efficiency) in the quadriceps of top cyclists than in those of marathon runners. These biopsies demonstrated to him that ability in one sport did not automatically equip one for top performance in another. He theorized that given only so many hours in a day, running would only deter cyclists from developing the crucial cell energy needed in their quadriceps.

No evidence exists that learning to swim 100 yards in record time will make you faster in the 100-yard dash. Simply put, a sports specialist who wishes to remain so, particularly at short distances, may not become faster by adopting other disciplines. In fact, he or she may add some detracting muscle mass that will actually cause slower times.

Other sports will improve your overall condition, however, so that you'll perform better aerobically for a longer time and with a keener sense of motor coordination, especially in *long-distance* events where endurance becomes the key. Cardiovascular conditioning transfers easily from one sport to another. It's the techniques that take time to learn.

Marc Surprenant, 22, a middle-distance champion triathlete from Centerville, Massachusetts, poses a prediction that years from now may obscure any current specificity-versus-multisport debate. "Eventually, you'll see triathletes who are able to turn in world-class performances in all events," he says. "That's the next step. Triathloning is so new that we're seeing athletes who come from specific training backgrounds. But pretty soon we'll have people who are 'elite' in swimming, cycling, and running because they'll have a long competitive background in all those areas."

By way of summary, cross-training differs from sport specialization in that it focuses on:

1. Reducing your risk of injury and keeping yourself in condition if you are already injured.

2. Improving your endurance capacity beyond single-sport levels.

3. Building both upper- *and* lower-body strength uniformly.

4. Developing your highest potential of overall conditioning and total fitness.

5. Avoiding the boredom of single-sports specificity by adding variety to your training.

6. Giving yourself a "beyond-a-marathon" challenge (although

many triathletes consider marathons tougher than multisport events of much longer distances).

7. Eventually developing high-quality training whereby *fewer hours* are spent working out—for *maximum* results.

Running into trouble

World-class cyclist John Howard got caught with a flat tire during a training ride at the 1976 Montreal Olympics. Since he was only 100 yards from Olympic Village, he decided to hoist his bicycle and run for it instead of changing the tire in the rain. He woke up so stiff the next morning that he wondered what had hit him. If running only 100 yards could inflict such damage, then maybe he wasn't in as great shape as he wanted to be. He was fit for cycling, but not fit overall. After that discovery, he altered his training radically and with such fervor that 5 years later he won the Ironman Triathlon World Championship.

An increasing number of runners sidelined with Achilles tendinitis, plantar fasciitis, shinsplints, and other afflictions are stumbling across the benefits of cross-training much the way Howard did. Have you ever tried to pacify injured runners denied their true passion? Without that constant infusion of endorphins, the body's natural-high, painkilling hormones, runners easily slip out of condition and into a very real depression. Finally, unable to restrain themselves—fish gotta swim, birds gotta fly—they take to the streets again and end up aggravating their old wounds and causing new ones.

Edward Donahue, a Santa Barbara physical therapist who deals with sports injuries, believes that expanded training can effectively treat what is becoming a new problem—sports addiction. "People continue to run despite injuries," he says, "because they feel that they can't give it up. I think alternative activities could save them from more harm, and yet allow them to remain active."

Dr. Edward Colt, a New York endocrinologist who specializes in treating running injuries, goes even further in the connection between sports addiction and multisport exercising. "The expanded-training explosion is a direct result of all those running injuries of the last decade," he says. "First came the diet explosion, followed by the exercise boom, with the marathon as the ultimate achievement. Now a new, more balanced renaissance athlete is evolving. We need an answer to all those running-impact trauma problems caused by continually forcing three times our body weight onto the road each time our foot strikes the ground. Running is the activity that most commonly results in impact trauma, whereas there is no impact in a fluid activity such as bicycling. Other types of training vary between these two extremes as regards impact or trauma to bones or joints."

Dr. Colt recommends cycling for injured runners. In addition to lessening your chances of injury by strengthening the entire structure of agonist and antagonist muscles in your legs, you'll find increased flexibility in the hip and knee joints, improved ability to run uphill, increased leg speed, and, of course, continued cardiovascular endurance.

"Any kind of exercise frequently helps another," adds Colt. For instance, he recommends shadowboxing to his patients who are racquetball players. "It makes them lighter on their feet and gives them the ability to move in many directions," he says. "It also strengthens the deltoids, which are necessary to maintain the integrity of the shoulder joints—a vulnerable area, of course, in all racquet sports."

For skiers, Colt prescribes static wall squats. "These aren't like deep knee bends, which I don't recommend at all, because the latter are so traumatic to the knee joints," he explains. "Instead, try wall squats, which consist of sitting against a wall, with your thighs horizontal and your legs vertical. Maintain the position for 3 minutes at a time by using your quadriceps. I use this as a treatment *and* as a test. A runner who can't do this for 3 minutes is likely to develop knee injuries. For such cases, I prescribe wall squats repeated six times per day until the runner can do it for 3 minutes at a time. Needless to say, wall squats are a great way to prepare for skiing."

"I started riding a bike because I had so much back pain while running," says Conrad Will, 42, of Del Mar, California. "While cycling has taken some speed away from my running because I'm developing the sort of muscle mass that makes me less fluid, it has definitely gotten rid of my back pains. I've also found that skiing helps my running form."

Vicky Zomar of the National Athletic Health Institute in Inglewood, California, agrees with the assessments of Donahue and Colt. "Expanded training is a significant rehabilitative aid," she says. "It also gives people who are not professional athletes a safe way to work out frequently, and it creates a system of substitutions." When you're out of the saddle because of chrondomalacia (knee problems), you can swim, and shoulder tendinitis won't interfere with running.

In addition to being a direct outgrowth of efforts by the relatively new field of sports medicine to treat injuries, expanded training is also used as preventive medicine. As far back as 1959, Sam Bell, track and cross-country coach at Indiana University, was directing his injured runners to the pool because of the water's cushioning effects. But they weren't always swimming. They'd wear ski vests or ski belts and actually run in the water. Since their feet never touched the ground, no pounding was involved.

The water's resistance made the work that much harder and more intense. Bell soon discovered that this higher intensity did more than just maintain their level of conditioning. In many cases the runners made greater progress in a shorter time than when they stuck solely to the track. Bell kept pool work as part of the regular running program.

Brooks Johnson, director of track and field at Stanford University, sends some of the best women distance runners in the world into the water—this time for actual swimming. Bill Dellinger, track and cross-country coach at the University of Oregon, shares Johnson's emphasis on learning new skills and breathing rhythms to maximize conditioning while avoiding injury. After successfully directing injured runners through repeated sprint sets in thigh-deep water, Dellinger made the pool work part of his team's regular routine—a not inappropriate move, considering that they're nicknamed "The Ducks."

Alternate sports will prevent injury as long as you proceed slowly at first. You may be in excellent cardiovascular condition, but your lack of specific mechanical skills in a new discipline may catch you unaware. Remember that you're stressing entirely new muscle groups and falling into unfamiliar rhythms. Whereas runners are accustomed to a great deal of pounding out on the road, swimmers and cyclists are used to pushing hard without risking injury. A swimmer can get hurt by summoning up that instinct while tired if he or she is running for the first time. Runners, meanwhile, will be busy adjusting to the biomechanical complexities of navigating through water.

As an accomplished runner put it when he took up cycling, in an echo of John Howard's sentiments, "I thought I was in top condition. So why am I hurting in places I never even knew I had?"

The improvement capacity

Learning to expand your endurance capacity and develop a sense of pacing first involves pushing through that feeling of being out of breath and working hard. "When you're new to aerobic exercise, you think, 'I'm going to die! This is it!' the minute your heart starts pounding," says triathlete and top marathoner JoAnn Dahlkoetter of San Francisco. "But that's where the real conditioning starts. You have to get used to that feeling. It's not pain. Your heart's not going to stop. You've reached that exhilarating point of feeling yourself getting into shape. Sustain that for a while during your first few workouts, and then stop. Cut it short, even. But build from there. Make it rewarding, and you've won the battle."

Converting this feeling into a relaxed, continuous effort instead of a struggle is an inner process that can take years. Triathletes soon realize that tensing up runs antithetical to the "letting go" required in endurance events. "It's not pain," insists Jann Girard. "I see it as just a variety of sensations."

Whether you call it "pain" or "sensations," the final result is eventually the same. Lactic acid and other metabolic waste products accumulate in the muscles during prolonged, oxygen-debt exercise. Fatigue sets in when the muscles cannot disperse the lactic acid into the bloodstream faster than the working muscles are producing it.

Cross-training eases the buildup of lactic acid by allowing different muscle groups to assume the continuing stress. As the early cross-education experiments demonstrated, when one muscle group begins to fatigue, bringing an inactive one into play can keep the tiring systems going longer, although not perhaps at overload intensity.

Triathletes can run until the lactic acid buildup in their legs prompts them to switch to the pool—where the muscles in their upper bodies are the prime workers—for continued aerobic conditioning and to stretch out. This cross-stress potential explains why many find it less taxing to complete a triathlon of greater-than-marathon distance than to run an unrelieved 26.2 miles.

It also explains why triathletes can work some 5 hours a day, whereas top marathon runners can only put in a few hours daily at the height of their training. The world's best triathletes can literally put in 8-hour days. No single-sport specialist could possibly take such intensity day in and day out. The body's skeletal system and tissues wouldn't cooperate.

Sustained aerobic performances as a result of combining sports has prompted the invention of cross-stress definitions. Sally Edwards defines *cross-bonking* as fatigue that strikes in one exercise but finally hits as you're pursuing another. For instance, exhaustion while swimming might knock you out halfway into an ensuing cycling leg. Cross-bonking represents supreme pace miscalculation. *Cross-peaking*, on the other hand, is optimum maneuvering through several consecutive sports segments. A triathlete at cross-peak is performing at a high-caliber endurance rhythm.

This vocabulary about cross-training has given rise to such idioms as *bike-to-run syndrome*. Sally Edwards describes it as the inability to run well after cycling, probably because of the shortening of the quadriceps that results from bicycling.

The best way to ward off any humbling syndromes is to remember that time is the great equalizer in triathloning. Dave Scott gave a prime example of cross-peaking when he broke his own world record at the 1983 Ironman World Championship without posting the fastest time in any of the three segments. (His times were the sixth fastest in swimming and second in both cycling and running.) He knew instead how to endure at the best tempo overall.

Swimmer's shoulders, cyclist's legs

Swimmers have impressive upper bodies; cyclists have those apocalyptic thighs; runners' sinewy frames belie powerful legs.

But triathletes develop each of these assets. While specialists may be more noticeable because of hyperdevelopment in the area specific to their sport, triathletes opt for uniformity and a high aerobic capacity—which isn't the exclusive province of any one body type.

In fact, contrary to what you might think, triathletes do not look overpowering—at least not until they spring into action. Some of the best of them, men and women, are surprisingly small and thin. (Leanness can be a problem in cold water, but anyone will tell you that too many layers of insulating fat are a real liability while running.) What they have is overall toughness—upper *and* lower body—and a look of total fitness.

Variations on a theme

Nothing makes a training program self-destruct faster than monotony or ennui. At the very least, an integration of different skills prevents you from losing touch with the reason for working out in the first place—the desire for lifelong fitness.

"Don't give up anything you're doing athletically. Add to it," says triathlete Julie Moss. "Keep going to your aerobics or jazzercise class. And I think yoga is great. My personal key to success is to enjoy my training, to combine it with everything else I'm doing. That's why I involve my friends and pleasant surroundings as much as possible."

Athletes bored with what they're doing have quite a different reaction to training. A seasoned pool competitor once complained to me that he took a 20-year hiatus from swimming because the smell of chlorine started making him sick. "I couldn't stand it," he said. "It smelled too much like work." His aversion might have been avoided entirely if he had allowed the relief of other sports into his routine.

Having alternate sports also keeps you in top condition when the weather interferes. Cross-training can prevent you from injuring yourself in your mad dashes to make up for lost time.

"You need other options, especially if you live in the Midwest or East," says Anne McDonnell, 21, of Minnesota. "I forget about running during the winter and ski all the time, and I ride a wind-load simulator (indoor cycling apparatus). When I'm ready to start running again, it's easier to build back into top form because I've kept up my aerobic work in other ways. If you can't run all year long, you need other plans or you'll go crazy."

Intensity + minimum time = maximum results

Many fitness athletes are not only bored by plodding through the same workout every day, doing the same distance of the same sport at the same pace; they're also not getting any better or faster—which leaves them with about as much enthusiasm for exercise as my chlorine-nauseated friend. They know that it's good for them, so they take their 50 laps or 10 miles like a pill and figure that maybe their confusing lack of improvement is a symptom of growing old, or else they tag on extra miles to make up for staying stuck on such a disappointing plateau.

Compare it to driving the same way home every day after work. An "automatic drive" sensation suddenly descends because the overly familiar has you virtually asleep at the controls. It's no different with exercise.

If success depends on how high the numbers are in your logbook, how can you ever escape the nagging feeling that somehow, if you really tried, you could do more? Even the venerable Kenneth Cooper recently asserted, "If you're running more than 15 miles a week, it's for something other than fitness."

A system is needed whereby you achieve maximum results in a minimum amount of time. Part 2 explains exactly why intensity exercise, interspersed with complete rest, eventually yields greater results than if you hope to improve solely on the basis of long-duration work. For one thing, intensity plus rest institutes a system of reward for hard work. It allows you to progress faster and accommodate several sports more effectively and efficiently.

Suffice it here to say that this formula shapes into a wonderfully freeing notion when employed in other areas of life as well. If, for example, you spend 10 hours writing a company brochure or building bookshelves that a higher degree of concentration could have powered out in 6, those extra hours are mostly your conviction that more time spent (long, slow distance work) translates automatically into a better product. Our ingrained work ethic makes it easy for us to confuse dawdling with dedication.

It's not how long you work that matters, in other words; it's how hard and with how apt a sense of direction.

A new frontier

The novelty of triathloning is an incentive. We are not talking about lone daredevils who storm across Death Valley. On a slow news day, they will always be among us. We're talking about a sports challenge in which you needn't be young or have a competitive background in order to succeed. You'll be able to include a wider range of people with a broader range of skills into your sphere by associating with the various Masters swimming groups, cycling clubs, and running associations in your area. These are the best places to learn training tips and to hear about races. With cross-training it's easy to feel that you belong to something formative and exciting—but not necessarily easy. The sport of triathloning is accessible, as we've seen, to those over 30 who remain strong on endurance. Women may eventually be able to compete in combination sports on a closer par with men than they might in single-sport events, and amateurs may be able to perform in a winning combination in ways they might not in a single test of skills.

Many people have been operating in the true spirit of cross-training for years. "I was a triathlete when I was a kid. It just didn't have a name," says Tom Warren, winner of the 1979 Ironman. "In 1953, I'd do my newspaper route for time on my bike, then race to the beach to body surf before running to school."

If you've always ascribed to an active life-style, cross-training will strike you as second nature. "I've been a triathlete since I was six," says northern California's perennial Escape From Alcatraz Triathlon winner Dave Horning. "I *just didn't know it.*"

Preservation of health is a duty. Few people seem to be
conscious of such a thing as physical morality.
—Hippocrates (c. 460–400 B.C.)

I was a telephone operator and sold classified ads before getting
married. After that I sold hotel pictures and hung advertisements on
the doors of homes until the dogs got too vicious for me. Eventually
my husband and I loaded into a Volkswagen bus and drove from
Florida to the West Coast. We picked fruit in Oregon, and then
ended up in Hawaii looking for similar work.

After a while as domestic help on Oahu, we saved up enough
money to buy a fitness center. My husband and I split up after
working together for a while. I was alone, on my own for the first
time in a long while, when John Collins asked me to put together
the first two Ironman Triathlons. I've never been athletic, but I like to
organize things. At first I thought it was nuts. But being married
hadn't worked, and neither had fitness centers. It was time for
something new.

Five days after my divorce was final, the first Ironman was staged.
It's been like a child to me ever since, a symbol of death and birth.
And now, years later and having watched the race mature, I feel it's
time for me to cut the umbilical cord and move on.

—Valerie Silk
Race director of the Ironman, on
moving to worldwide Ironman
promotion in 1984

CHAPTER 2

From Naked Pentathletes to Ironmen: An informal history of multisport events

The best thing about good ideas is that they always resurface. Lately we've taken to dusting off the old concepts of sports versatility and endurance—notions as old as Euripides—to find relief from the drive of the past years toward specialization.

Specialization was certainly the buzzword when I was in college a few years back. The horizon was so vast, the reasoning went, that unless we split up and attacked it piecemeal, all the work or possible athletic feats stretching before us would never get done. We graduated with our chosen fields divided into many interlocking parcels.

This works fairly well in theory—at least until obsolescence breeds expendability. Where do you go when your area of expertise is outmoded? A more holistic approach creates options.

Dr. Edward Colt believes that our rediscovered emphasis on balance and the need for alternatives in athletics marks a return to the Greek ideal of the well-rounded person. "That's because sports are no longer as health-giving as they should be," he says. "Professionalism and the emphasis on money destroy athletes who aren't equipped to deal with that sort of pressure. Ten years ago, the idea behind the marathon was just to finish. Now everyone's obsessed with timing.

"That's how the Greeks started out. Moderation was their goal in everything, but when they started the Olympics, they became terribly competitive. They lost sight of their reasons for encouraging the games in the first place.

"That's happening now, because it's pretty bad in most sports. Athletes often push themselves beyond their limits, to the point of self-destruction. For example, the average lifespan of professional football players is shorter than that of the general population. Triathlons and multisport training indicate that we are recognizing the need for less competition—a reemphasis on finishing, not winning. Sports may once more be evolving back into a gentlemanly pursuit designed to attain health and promote camaraderie."

Sacrificial rams

Those first Olympic Games integrated physical, religious, and intellectual paeans into one massive spectacle. Prayers, hymns, and religious ceremonies, complete with black rams sacrificed on altars, supposedly appeased any gods still upset about the head-on collisions during the chariot races.

No one combined skill, strength, and versatility more supremely during these games than the pentathletes, who so exemplified the Greek notion of physical beauty that they performed naked under the sun. Poets and sculptors could scarcely restrain themselves. Even Aristotle concluded that a multisport event such as the pentathlon, introduced in 708 B.C., created "the most beautiful creatures in the world" because it demanded exercises of both speed and skill.

Versatility won the prize. First the pentathletes threw the discus and the javelin. After that came a standing broad jump, in which they carried weights in their hands to swing shoulder-high as they leaped. The weights increased the distance and helped the jumpers maintain their balance. A 200-meter sprint and a wrestling contest followed, unless someone had already won the first three contests to claim the title.

We shouldn't get carried away with grand notions about Greek ideals. We automatically ascribe nobility to ancient scenarios, forgetting that styles change with greater alacrity than human nature. The "most beautiful creatures in the world" were also mercilessly taunted if they lacked enough intelligence to balance their athleticism. The playwright Euripides, for example, was particularly unsparing when describing his muscular compatriots, insisting that once athletes aged they were "like old coats that have lost their resilience." One poor young jock named Milo of Croton was enough of a lummox to fuel "mindless-athlete" barbs for years. When Milo carried the carcass of a bull around the stadium at Olympia before feasting on it, writers went wild. "What surpassing witlessness" was the tamest attack. Several others pointed out that if the bull had been alive it would have carried itself around the stadium with a good deal more grace and far less exertion than Milo had.

That aside, the Greeks enjoyed a good show, even by someone like Milo, as much as anybody. What they objected to was his inability to answer the barbs. They had precious little appetite for esoteric and overworked skills, because they equated narrowness of focus with narrow-mindedness. It was no accident that they held important lectures in gymnasiums. They insisted, as Plato once declared, that the body and mind had to be "duly harmonized," and that gymnastic pursuits were the "twin sisters" of the arts for the "improvement of the soul." When someone broke rank by hyperdevelopment of one area to the exclusion of all others, they felt their creed of well-roundedness under attack.

Their criteria of sports excellence—strength, speed, stamina, and agility—now apply to the modern decathlon. Jim Thorpe of the United States won the first modern decathlon at the 1912 Olympic Games, but his eventual label of "world's greatest athlete" was not so much because of his record as because of his seemingly boundless skills in football, boxing, swimming, and numerous other sports.

Over the years such decathlon stars as Bob Mathias, Rafer Johnson, and Bruce Jenner have beaten Thorpe's record, demonstrating once again that we continually raise the ceiling on what we call "the greatest." Evolution is a fluid motion from which we select the most inspirational high points.

Fewer chores = evolution of fitness

Multisport events are a further extrapolation of the ways we use our leisure time. According to Robert H. Boyle's *Sport—Mirror of American Life*, by the end of 1939 the average worker had one more day of free time per week than he or she had in 1929, and two more than an 1890 counterpart. With more money and time to spend, people often turned to professional sports for entertainment.

For the most part, however, people *watched* sports. And sports meant *team* sports in the first half of this century. It wasn't until the 1960s that fitness became the widely acknowledged responsibility of each person.

A number of forces shaped the fitness boom. Cigarette smoking was linked to cancer. Doctors blamed obesity for a myriad of ailments, including cardiac problems. In 1968, Dr. Kenneth Cooper's best-selling *Aerobics* turned sports decisively from an assortment of team activities with national audiences into a prescription for everyone's health. Millions paid Cooper heed by running. It was accessible, economical, an excellent cardiovascular conditioner, and a great source of camaraderie.

Things started picking up in the other triathlon sports as well. Robert Boyle suggests that American swimmers made such impressive showings during the 1972 and 1976 Olympics that swimming, already one of the country's top participatory sports, began riding a new crest. And, as we've already seen, it gave injured runners new options.

As for cycling, it had always been a popular sport in Europe but not in America, where the car has been a status symbol, and scarce or inadequate public transport over vaster distances has kept bicycling a low-key pastime or Sunday afternoon diversion. But by the early 1970s, during widespread gas shortages and the antipollution movement, 10 million bicycles were manufactured in the United States, surpassing the total number of cars produced in the same time period.

By the end of the 1970s, swimming, running, and cycling claimed an impressive 63.7 million active participants—meaning those who engaged in the sport at least once a week. A 1961 survey by the President's Council on Physical Fitness showed that 24 percent of U.S. citizens exercised at least three times a week, but a 1983 survey by Miller Lite disclosed that 44 percent of the country engaged in at least one athletic activity a day. The Miller Lite Report on American Attitudes Toward Sports also showed that 90 percent of all active fitness athletes enjoy one or more of triathloning's three major sports. The combined percentage indicates a high degree of cross-training already.

Most Popular Participation Sports*

	Daily or Almost Daily	About Once or Twice a Week	Total
Swimming	13	20	33
Calisthenics	15	14	29
Jogging	12	17	29
Bicycling	13	15	28
Softball/baseball	7	14	21
Weight lifting	6	9	15
Basketball	6	8	14
Football/rugby	4	8	12
Tennis, squash, etc.	3	9	12
Pool/billiards	3	8	11

*In percentages. Number of respondents—1319.

SOURCE: MILLER LITE REPORT ON AMERICAN ATTITUDES TOWARD SPORTS.

Cross-country skiing, which physiologists acknowledge as the best overall fitness exercise, deserves a special note of praise. The arm swinging and the substantial agility and weaving required of a skier's legs combine to make it a perfect upper- and lower-body exercise. Coordination and a sense of balance enter in.

Along with swimming, cycling, and running, cross-country skiing ranks as one of the best possible calorie-burning and cardiovascular conditioners. For most of us, though, skiing is a distant passion. Between the capriciousness of snowy weather and the expense of travel, very few of us can parlay skiing into year-round training. It is nevertheless a superior aerobic exercise and the most common cold-climate substitute for swimming in a triathlon.

Putting it all together

Multisport events—some organized, some impromptu—hit the West Coast well over 20 years ago, as lifeguards, surfers, and diehard ocean swimmers squared off against each other. "I remember something called the Ironman out here in Southern California when I was 16," says triathlete Bill Leach, 37. "Lifeguards would swim, surfboard paddle, dory paddle (in the rowboatlike crafts they used on the job), and then run."

The term "Ironman" was actually coined in Australia in the early 1900s to lament the end of the windjammer era, the time of the "wooden ships and iron men." By the twenties, Australian lifeguards had appropriated "Ironman" to describe their swimming, board paddling, and dory rowing contests—a notion which eventually hit the California coast.

But Australians and Californians live so much out in the open that it was impossible to keep ocean swimming a private party forever. As thousands took the rough-water plunge, organized

HARALD JOHNSON

Ocean races and biathlons—such as the Avila Beach Swim-Run-Swim shown here—soon evolved into triathlons and other multisport events.

ocean races gained enough popular appeal to prompt a need for new tests of skill.

One such contest was the annual TUG's Swim-Run-Swim, initiated in 1974 by Tom Warren, owner of TUG's, a San Diego tavern. Warren went on to win the 1979 Ironman title, and multievent races matured far beyond being simply a day at the beach.

On July 27, 1974, Eppie's Great Race in Sacramento went into the books as the first official relay triathlon. Fifty-two three-person teams ran 10 miles, maneuvered a watercraft (kayak, raft, or canoe) 2 miles across the American River, and bicycled back 4.7 miles to the beer and hot dogs waiting at Eppie's Restaurant. Ten-speed bicycles, rafts, and jogging outfits were awarded to first-, second-, and third-place teams, respectively.

The May 1975 Fiesta Island Race in Mission Bay, near San Diego, became the first recorded triathlon in which participants competed in all three events. Bill Phillips, now an exercise physiologist at San Diego State University, won the ½-mile swim, 5-mile cycle, and 5-mile run ahead of 21 others. The contest took place a mere two months before the second annual Eppie's Great Race had its first athlete take on all three segments—Pax Beale, the first man to swim from Alcatraz Island at night.

"He saw the trend and told us to get with it," says Eppie's race

Cyclists await the start of Eppie's Great Race at an early event. Cyclists now compete in the second stage of the run, bike, paddle event.

director Chuck Woodbury. Eppie's tenth annual race, held in 1983 (a 6.5-mile run, 12.5-mile bike ride, and 6.35-mile paddle) makes it the world's oldest continuous triathlon.

The true larger-than-life extravaganza that finally sanctioned the new trend was the Hawaiian Ironman Triathlon World Championship (2.4-mile swim, 112-mile cycle, and 26.2-mile run).

Welcome to the iron age

One night in 1977, ex-Navy captain and Waikiki Swim Club member John Collins, now 42, started a good-natured argument with some friends in a Honolulu bar over who was the fittest—the swimmer, cyclist, or runner. They battled over the merits of Oahu's three existing endurance events—the 2.4-mile Waikiki Rough Water Swim, the Honolulu Marathon, and the Around-Oahu Bicycle Race (then a two-day event).

That's when Collins came up with a real conversation stopper: string them together, and let's see who walks their talk. "I had no idea the Ironman was going to grow so fast," Collins later said.

The dare was unreasonable enough to intrigue 15 men to enter the groundbreaking race in February 1978. Gordon Haller, 27, won in 11:46:58. The next year, 14 men and one woman, Lyn Lemaire of Boston, competed. Tom Warren took over a half an hour off the record.

Warren hit a certain nerve when he commented in a follow-up *Sports Illustrated* article that the money he'd spent for the trip had been well worth it. "Some people would take the $1000 and buy furniture, but this is something you'll have with you for the rest of your life," he said.

By 1980, the barroom dare was shaping a fitness frontier. It was turning out to be an idea of the right time and place. Hawaii's half-hallucinatory air added the requisite glamorous backdrop— this is, after all, where parakeets fly through the tropical steam that nurtures orchids. That year two women and 106 men entered a race won handily by Dave Scott. Robin Beck of Utah took over an hour and a half off Lemaire's record.

What was keeping such an unwieldly contest an athletic holy grail? "When someone tells me something is impossible," offers Dave Horning in partial explanation, "that makes me want to do it even more."

Race director Valerie Silk had some decisions to make. "It was getting too big too fast to be safe on Oahu," she said. "I moved it to the big island of Hawaii."

A judicious move, because in 1981, 356 entrants waded into Kailua Bay in Kona, a big enough crowd to convince Budweiser Light to enlist as a sponsor for the following year. After John Howard and Linda Sweeney won the 1981 race, Silk and her organizers decided to stage one last Ironman the following February before switching the race to October to allow triathletes more time and better weather for training. There would therefore be two races in 1982.

The Ironman had a reputation as a race of such exhaustive detail—down to the correct number of fresh leis waiting at the finish line—that although lack of a prize purse kept it amateur, it seemed more professional than professional triathlons. The layout of the grand concourse was so skillful that spectators could glimpse a part of every stage of the race. For the world's best triathletes, it was tantamount to graduation day at the end of a long season. "The Ironman? That's the easy part," says triathlete Colin Brown. "If you get through all those long months of training, this is the party."

Even without prize money, the emotional payoff was getting higher all the time. "The race and I seemed so fused together that I wondered if one of us could have survived without the other," says Silk.

Even Silk could not have predicted the emotional fallout of the fifth Ironman. On February 6, 1982, 584 triathletes watched the sunrise turn the sky lavender beyond the steeple of Mokuaikaua Church, waiting for the cannon blast that would start the race.

Most wanted only to finish, but a few planned to take the lava fields of Queen Kaahumanu Highway by storm. It wasn't going to be easy. The sun and weight of the humidity could be almost as devastating as the gale-force winds on a cycling route as barren as moonscape, if not for those occasional coral-colored wildflowers that offered the only relief to the eye.

One of those with a grand notion was Scott Tinley, the eventual winner over his arch rival Dave Scott. Tinley's 40-hour training weeks had always kept him high on the circuit, and on that day he was unbeatable. He punched in a 9:19:41 to win decisively.

As Tinley was recovering on a massage table from his ordeal, the ABC-TV cameras were rolling, unmindful that a story that commentators would later extol as one of the most exciting in sports history was approaching. If ever there was a moment that not only gave a sport the stamp of validity but skyrocketed it into a fitness passion, it was right around the corner. Populist triathloning was about to be born.

Eleven hours into the race, Julie Moss, a 23-year-old from Carlsbad, California, collapsed 2 miles from the finish line. She had taken a substantial lead in the women's race during the last 5 miles, a push that had her wobbling and swaying during her final march down Kona's Alii Drive. The cameras zoomed in. The ensuing, much-ballyhooed loss of her bodily functions—to give it a discreet turn of phrase—was recorded on film. Her legs offered no support, and the enormity of the event finally brought her to her knees.

Or at least it tried to. That's when Moss summoned up the reserves that make crowds go wild. There was plenty of screaming. Officials were screaming at the bystanders that if they touched her she would be disqualified. Bystanders were screaming that she needed help. She refused all help and started crawling the final 15 yards to the finish line.

Just then, Kathleen McCartney, from La Jolla, who had been relentlessly making up the 21-minute deficit Moss had handed her during the swim that morning, blazed through the strobe lights and passed Moss's outstretched hand for the women's crown. It took Julie Moss another 20 seconds to inch those last few feet and register 11:10:09. She later called it her "study in collapse."

No ad agency could have staged a more incredible pas de deux to make triathloning a household word. McCartney did the Carson show. They both appeared on "Today." Interviews, magazine covers, more talk shows, and limousines to go shopping in New York followed.

Some athletes complained that the limelight belonged to those whose dedication, skills, and preparation would always preclude any staggering around. But if human nature admires excellence, it becomes enamored with a compelling story, especially when underdogs play the leads. Two ordinary women with scant athletic histories had made it to the top. Far from the blood-and-guts spectacle being off-putting, it struck that innate desire in everyone to emerge from obscurity by "going the distance."

The tide rose even higher. That October, Dave Scott mastered the course over 849 other triathletes with such finesse that the day was his unchallenged from the moment a snapped bicycle derailleur canceled Mark Allen's chances. Until the mechanical breakdown, Allen had been keeping pace with Scott. Julie Leach set a new women's record and led JoAnn Dahlkoetter, Sally Edwards, and Kathleen McCartney across the finish line.

Silk instituted a qualification system to deal with the deluge of applicants. She decided to limit the 1983 race to 1000 entrants. A crayoned letter that read, "We love our Daddy. Please let him be an Ironman!" was all the evidence she needed that word was traveling fast.

In 1983, Dave Scott and Scott Tinley staged a down-to-the-wire finish that converted an all-day endurance event into a virtual sprint for the finish. Dave Scott won his third title by 33 seconds—the sort of margin you'd expect in a footrace. The event was later seen on ABC's "Wide World of Sports" by well over 12 million households, giving the popular show its highest rating in 3 years. Over 7000 applications were sent out for the 1000 slots available in the 1984 race.

Other developments were shaping up in the rest of the pack. Kathleen McCartney did not finish among the top 10 women, and Julie Moss was even further behind. The day belonged instead to two newcomers, 22-year-old Montreal twins Sylviane and Patricia Puntous. Sally Edwards, 36, placed in the top five women again, as she had in the past three races. Edwards had always skipped over dramatic splashes and stuck to serious business. Her persistent high performances are in contrast to the fate of most Ironman entrants. Very few athletes—including winners such as McCartney and Moss—can keep up the rugged pace required to compete in the Ironman year after year.

Many top competitors have their eyes on a fledgling professional circuit and see the Ironman, in Tinley's words, as "the one Olympic event, the torch race of the sport where there's a lot more going for it than money." The Ironman remains the showcase, however; potential sponsors are interested in how an elite triathlete does in the Ironman.

For those who have no vision of earning a livelihood from triathloning, the solution often has been concentrating on more manageable distances. "Unlike most sports, the triathlon was built from the top down. Not from the bottom up," explains Tom Patty, a Los Angeles advertising executive who participates in medium-distance triathlons. "First there was the Hawaiian Iron-

A Cross-Training Tour

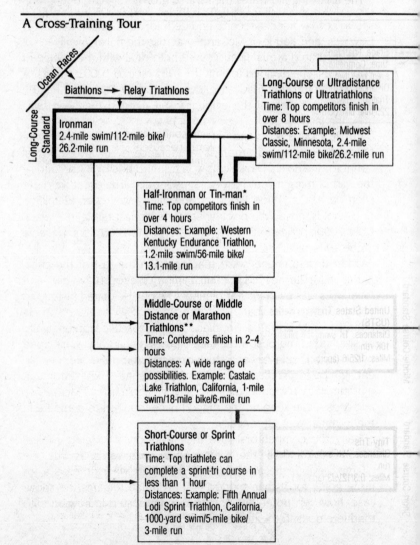

Ocean Races

Long-Course Standard

Biathlons → Relay Triathlons

Ironman
2.4-mile swim/112-mile bike/
26.2-mile run

Long-Course or Ultradistance Triathlons or Ultratriathlons
Time: Top competitors finish in over 8 hours
Distances: Example: Midwest Classic, Minnesota, 2.4-mile swim/112-mile bike/26.2-mile run

Half-Ironman or Tin-man*
Time: Top competitors finish in over 4 hours
Distances: Example: Western Kentucky Endurance Triathlon, 1.2-mile swim/56-mile bike/ 13.1-mile run

Middle-Course or Middle Distance or Marathon Triathlons**
Time: Contenders finish in 2–4 hours
Distances: A wide range of possibilities. Example: Castaic Lake Triathlon, California, 1-mile swim/18-mile bike/6-mile run

Short-Course or Sprint Triathlons
Time: Top triathlete can complete a sprint-tri course in less than 1 hour
Distances: Example: Fifth Annual Lodi Sprint Triathlon, California, 1000-yard swim/5-mile bike/ 3-mile run

man. Then came national television exposure on ABC's 'Wide World of Sports.' And *then* came the proliferation of short- and medium-distance races. It's like having the Super Bowl without the prior existence of college football teams or the World Series without first having Little League baseball."

The following illustrates the inverse growth of triathloning.

Stage Triathlons
Time: Competitors complete the event over two or more days
Distances: Example: Big Island Triathlon, Hawaii, 6-mile swim/225-mile bike/50-mile run

Professional Triathlons

Middle-Course Standard

United States Triathlon Series (USTS)
Distances: 1K swim/40K bike/10K run
Miles: 1/25/6 (approx.)

Short-Course Standard

Tiny Tris
Distances: ½K swim/20K bike/5K run
Miles: 0.3/12½/3 (approx.)

Non-competitive Cross-Training

Although there have been some attempts to establish standard triathlon distances—a necessary step before they can be considered Olympic events—there are no recognized ratios. That's partly because as of 1984 no official governing body has complete control over the sport, and partly because it is impossible to compare a 30-mile hilly cycling course in Vermont, for example, with a 30-mile flat course in Oregon.

The debate over what ratios constitute a "balanced" triathlon—one in which the swimmer, cyclist, and runner have an equal chance of winning—also continues. (The boxes denote the most notable attempts by organizations to establish long-, middle- and short-course standards.) The consensus is that the sport is growing in every suitable direction, with athletes interested in noncompetitive cross-training on the one hand, and high-caliber professional triathletes on the other.

*Some athletes consider *every* triathlon that is not Ironman length to be a "Tin-man."

**Marathon triathlons are so-called because they generally take as long to complete as a 26-mile run.

This sampler of a few of the 1000 races held in 1983 demonstrates how the sport has evolved.

Bonne Bell Women's Triathlon, *May, Redwood Shores, CA, 1K swim, 30K bike, 10K run*. A Marine World elephant rang the bell that propelled almost 1000 women across a lagoon. Over 70 percent of the participants were first-time triathletes.

Bear Valley Triathlon, *May, Near Lake Tahoe, CA, 4-mile run, 8-mile bike, 6-mile cross-country ski*. Temperatures soared into the 80s as skiers clad only in bathing suits plowed over 10 feet of snowpack high in the Sierras.

Triathlon Dallas, *June, Dallas, TX, 1-mile swim, 43-mile bike, 10-mile run*. Over 600 participated in a race so well organized that they received aerial maps of the course in their prerace packages.

Maine Event, *July, Gardiner, ME, 10K run, 7-mile canoe, 28-mile bike*. The rain in Maine plainly got stayed as local running, cycling, and canoeing clubs teamed up in perfect weather to stage the state's first triathlon.

Sunkist Triathlon, *July, Oxnard, CA, 1-mile swim, 10-mile bike, 4-mile run*. It was an authentic, family-style triathlon. Local merchants sold barbecued chickens and homebaked goods as 200 triathletes (400 had applied) entered the race. Entrants found that they all finished with plenty of time to spend at the sports festival held concurrently in an adjoining park.

Mighty Hamptons, *July, Sag Harbor, NY, 1.5-mile swim, 25-mile bike, 10-mile run*. This one has it all: pine forests, countryside, marshes—and enough organization to make it one of the crown jewels on the eastern circuit. It's within driving distance of most major northeastern cities. Most of the 600 entrants last year were participating in their first triathlon.

WAAY-31-TV Triathlon, *August, Huntsville, AL, 3-mile run, 6-mile bike, 400-meter swim*. This triathlon exemplified the shorter distances that have introduced thousands of novices across the country to cross-training and a day at the races.

Levi's Ride and Tie, *August, Eureka, CA*. Horses get in on the act in this unusual triathlon that involves 43 miles of distance running, endurance horsemanship, and ride-and-tie skills up in the redwood forests.

Bachman Center Triathlon for the Handicapped, *August, Dallas, TX, Short Course: 1.5 miles rowing a two-person inflatable raft, 3.1-mile push around the jogging path, half-mile swim in a local indoor pool. Long Course: double the distances.* Efforts here and in other triathlons on behalf of handicapped athletes encouraged race directors elsewhere to follow suit.

Horny Toad Invitational, *August, San Diego, CA, 1.5-mile swim, 50-mile bike, 13.1-mile run.* This invitation-only triathlon is designed for elite performers, and the purple and green clothes worn by volunteers—not to mention the purple Nikes worn for the event by the athletes—evince a camaraderie worthy of special note.

Steel Man, *September, Brattleboro, VT, 60.6-mile bike, 10.3-mile run, 10.2-mile canoe.* Flat roads, rolling hills, and a few hard uphill grades for good measure kept cyclists at work in the green mountains of Vermont.

Nice (France) International Triathlon, *September, 3K swim, 100K bike, 30K run.* The world's top triathletes enter this slightly-under-Ironman-distance race. Mark Allen and Linda Buchanan, both of California, won in 1983. With $75,000 in prize money, including $10,000 each to Allen and Buchanan, this is the richest triathlon to date, although a number of potential money-makers are on the horizon for the 1984 season, indicating that a certain class of professional triathlete is developing and that the sport is receiving international notice.

Sextathlon, *January, Waikiki, HI, 500-yard swim, 3-mile run, 18 holes golf, team round robin sand volleyball, 500-yard paddle, outrigger canoe, individual round robin racquetball.* This gentleman's race proves that even stranger mutations of triathloning are on the horizon.

United States Triathlon Series. *1.2-mile swim, 25-mile bike, 9-mile run.* In 1981, Carl Thomas, a vice-president of marketing for Speedo International, decided to design safe but demanding courses for novice triathletes across the United States. Jim Curl stepped in as the main race director, and the result was a circuit that set a standard of safety, scenic routes, and organization by which most other medium-distance triathlons are now judged.

In 1982, the USTS staged five races on a city-to-city tour, and in 1983 it expanded to include Tampa, Atlanta, New York, San Francisco, Austin, Los Angeles, Chicago, San Diego, Seattle, Boston, Portland, and Bass Lake (near Yosemite) for the series championship. Tens of thousands of first-time triathletes participated. Prize money was awarded to the top places and plaques to age-group winners. Even shorter distances were planned for 1984 (1.5K swim, 40K bike, 10K run, approximately 1, 25, 6 in miles), to encourage more novices to join in.

For information on the USTS and other triathlons, consult sports publications, particularly those specializing in triathlon coverage, training camps, or governing bodies on the sport (see Appendix for lists of magazines, training camps, and organizations). Your local YMCA, YWCA, or sports clubs are also good sources.

PART 2

A Cross-Training Manual for Novices

Bite on the bullet, old man, and don't let them think you're afraid!

—Rudyard Kipling (1865–1936)

I needed my own Olympics to celebrate how fitness has changed me these last few years. Without it I'd be your typical, hard-working guy, still at IBM after 25 years. But cross-training was waking me up to a sense of balance that I desperately needed in the rest of my life. I wanted to save my 23-year marriage and find a way to talk with my four college-age kids.

That's why I invented my own triathlons every week for a year when I turned 50, and everything and everyone around me changed. I took a new and more challenging job as the vice president of ITM, a microcomputer firm, and my relationship with my wife, LaVerne, is the best it's ever been. I'd go so far as to credit the way being fit has taught me to relax and have fun with saving my marriage. Now that I feel healthy and alive, I'm no longer just an image to my kids, either. For the first time they see me as a person. They'll invite my wife and me to go dancing, and sometimes I can stay out on the floor longer than all of them. It's given me the courage to redesign the next 50 years of my life.

—Jack Riley, 52, Alamo, CA
Vice-president,
microcomputer firm

CHAPTER 3

Eleven Rules
of the cross-training
game

A preamble

You've heard the following disclaimer so many times it doubtless has the ring of all those what-to-do-when-the-oxygen-masks-unfurl lectures that some of you let go in one ear and out the other as the airplane prepares for takeoff. It's a lifesaving matter nonetheless.

Never let any fitness program substitute for either the advice of your physician or your own capabilities. If you are 35 or over or have a family history of cardiac problems, undergo a complete yearly physical, including a treadmill stress test and EKG reading, before any involvement in endurance training and regularly thereafter. Millions of cases of undiagnosed heart disease exist these days; angina pains are not always the precursors of a dangerous condition. Be *particularly cautious of any "overload" work (the interval options discussed in this section)*. High-stress work should be attempted only by those with a high degree of athletic proficiency.

Finally, noncompetitive cross-trainers might find complete yearly physicals a perfect way to appraise "personal best" progress. My friend Neil Feineman, for instance, submits to an annual battery of tests at the ALTA Fitness Institute in Los Angeles. This year they awarded him their green "Endurance Athlete" T-shirt (ALTA estimates only 5 percent of the population could qualify)—a leap from his blue "Aerobic Achiever" shirt (encompassing 25 percent of the population) the year before. He was as pleased as if he'd won a finisher's medal in the Ironman.

Now for the blueprint. This chapter will explain how to:

1. Establish an aerobic base, or a foundation of mileage.
2. Calculate formulas to discover the heart rate you should be targeting for best results.
3. Monitor your progress to avoid both undertraining and overtraining.
4. Avoid aimless training by focusing on *time* instead of *distance*. This may be the most vital upheaval in your athletic awareness that you'll make as a cross-trainer.
5. Develop other athletic "gears," or varied training speeds, to hasten your progress.
6. Combine different sports in the same workout to promote a sense of triathloning as *one sport, not three,* which will give you a tremendous psychological boost in budgeting your time and in declaring yourself a triathlete instead of a suddenly overwhelmed single-sport specialist.

Although cross-training is neither limited to nor defined by swimming, cycling, and running, those will be our sports of choice because they cover both upper- and lower-body development and are far and away the most popular endurance disciplines, as well as the most common events in multisport races. *Triathloning* as I use it here will mean the cross-training system that emphasizes those three sports.

Considering the different goals, aptitudes, and athletic credentials everyone brings to cross-training, it's impossible to spell out an airtight prescription that will work for everyone. To establish a point of departure, I dug up some demographics compiled by *Triathlon* magazine to sketch a median profile of potential cross-trainers.

A Cross-Trainer's Census

Primary Sports/Athletic Background

Cycling   6%
Swimming 22
Running   57
Other   15

Member of Sports Club

Swimming club 30%
Cycling club   19
Running club   46
Triathlon club 5

Participated in Sports Events

	None	1–4	5 or more
1-mile swim race	66%	19%	15%
50-mile cycle race	66	24	10
10K running race	11	22	66
Marathon running race	45	33	22

SOURCE: 1984 *TRIATHLON* MAGAZINE SURVEY.

Most novice triathletes:

1. Come from a running background.
2. Have entered several 10K races, and perhaps a marathon.
3. Probably took some swimming lessons as a child.
4. Have minimal cycling experience (the bike is collecting dust in the garage).
5. Are in their early 30s (male) or mid-20s (female).
6. Hold down full-time jobs.

Most dossier-derived compilations bear absolutely no resemblance to any living person. In this case, though, our fictional description fits my friend Brad Munson, a science-fiction writer, magazine veteran, and committed runner, practically down to his shoelaces.

Brad and I agreed that the Bonne Bell Triathlon held in 1983 near San Francisco had the perfect goal distances for beginners: 1K swim, 30K bike, 10K run (approximately ½, 20, 6 miles, respectively). We picked it as our sample model race based on the following:

1. The Bonne Bell race had more participants (almost 1000) than virtually any other triathlon ever held, and its success was largely because of its dimensions. Had the "women-only" stipulation been lifted, we thought the response would have been astronomical.

2. These distances are manageable for average-fitness athletes, allowing them to finish their first triathlon tired and challenged but with a sense of accomplishment.

3. The mileage is accessible to beginners who eventually want to spend only an hour exercising, five or six days a week.

4. Swimming is the most cumbersome of the three for adult athletes to pick up. Brad, who suffered through swimming lessons as a child only because his mother was convinced he would fall out of a boat someday, thought that half a mile was reasonable without being threatening.

5. Brad's goal-finishing time of around 3 hours (the top women in the Bonne Bell race finished in just under 2) is excellent marathon time, a frame of reference with which a novice with a running background can identify. More skilled athletes might need to make their lives somewhat tougher, and those just starting out with exercise will need more breathing room.

Starting Out:
Techniques and innovations

Now's the time to:

1. Join sports clubs to work with coaches and other athletes and to enjoy their camaraderie. Don't go it alone.

2. Assess your fitness goals.

3. Learn stroke mechanics, the latest techniques, and training tips.

4. Buy necessary equipment.

RULE 1:
Learn from experts first

Remember the Palmer method of handwriting? Students would trace archetypal letters over and over, trying to absorb perfect form. Presumably they should have ended up with similar writing instead of having such divergent styles that the only thing left in common was leaving Palmer in the dust.

Likewise, your cross-training style will evolve into a flashy personal autograph only, as they say in ice-skating, if you can trace your school figures first. "Learn the correct way when you start out," says Scott Tinley, "and then you'll develop your own signature." However, he points out, "I see a lot of guys fighting what comes naturally because they're stuck on imitating someone else's form. If something doesn't work for you, throw it out the window."

If you're a swimmer who's never cycled before, of course, you shouldn't pedal out of the showroom and down the highway with breakneck élan. An experienced cyclist or coach will save you plenty of later backpedaling by teaching you to choose one of many possible unknown quantities—to concentrate on the upstroke portion of your pedaling (consciously pulling from the 6 o'clock position up to 12 o'clock, not merely riding the momentum back), which doesn't come as instinctively or easily as the downstroke (pushing from 12 o'clock down to 6).

Don't thrash gamely ahead, thinking that you'll smooth out all the rough edges as you go along. Unlearning a mistake is tougher than starting with painful slowness. Bombard your response systems with basic patterns until skills become second nature. If you are in good cardiovascular condition but are learning a new sport, expect to feel awkward as you deliberately slow down in order to absorb what amounts to a foreign body language.

"**Remember that good form can tip the scales when you're exhausted,**" says triathlete Bob Curtis. "Sometimes that's all you've got left to carry you across the finish line."

Save time and sharpen your skills faster by having someone knowledgeable point out strategic corrections that might take you months to discover on your own. "Remember that technique is more important in some sports than in others," warns

Tinley. You can get along fine without a personal running coach, but don't attempt to master swimming solo. Getting the maximum possible energy efficiency out of every move is what you're after, not just covering the distance.

Although your local sports clubs, colleges, Masters programs, YMCAs, and YWCAs are packed to the gills with single-sport experts, coaches authoritative in more than one sport are harder to find. There are a few triathloning clinics and consultants around, but not everyone who completes a triathlon automatically becomes an expert on how you should train. A surgeon who performed a tonsillectomy is better versed in procedure than the patient who underwent the knife.

"Be wary of people who insist that what worked for them must work for you," says Tom Warren. "Athletics is an art form, and artists can't be told how to do anything. Be creative. Keep educating yourself. The only rule is that the harder you work, the luckier you get."

Inform any coaches or athletes you work with that you are triple-training. You'll save time and give your training direction. A swimming instructor, for example, would then help you refine your freestyle rather than teach you the butterfly.

"Learn to listen to your body," says Mark Allen. "What it tells you should always take precedence over any schedules. If I'm reluctant for any reason before a workout, I won't go ahead with it."

RULE 2:
Acquire a feel for each sport

Alberto Salazar's feet seem to float over the ground when he runs. Top athletes perform in a high-powered trance and make the incredible look effortless (as in, "Vladimir Salnikov is such a great swimmer he makes it look easy").

They know a tough task isn't made easier by struggling. World-class talents approach their medium with respect, not as conquering heroes who need to battle the road, water, or bicycle into submission.

That takes too much energy. Power comes from actually relaxing and sustaining internal focus. Since cross-training involves plunging yourself into unfamiliar environments and methods, developing this sense of nonresistance and being caught up in the moment—instead of gritting your teeth and barreling through—will speed up the learning process.

RULE 3:
Construct your own multisport events

When triathlete Jack Riley failed to find enough triathlons to meet his one-per-week goal in celebration of his 50th birthday, he invented his own series. His Masters swimming coach certified all his races to add a stamp of authenticity, and Riley christened them to add official color. His "Soggy Triathlon" (5.5-mile run, 22-mile bike, 1-mile swim) occurred during a northern California rainstorm. He finished in 3:03. In another race, he tagged very short swimming and running sprints onto the Davis Double Century Cycling Race, ending up with a 1-mile run, 164-mile bike, ¼-mile swim. He dubbed an agonizing 4.5-mile run, 22-mile bike, 1.5-mile swim his "Wine Triathlon" because of "too much partying the night before."

Devise your own informal triathlons, or add the missing segments onto official swimming, cycling, or running races. Such independent productions are an excellent way of practicing transitions, simulating actual race conditions, and providing a cross-training forum for others. The bottom line is that if you can't find contests that suit, live the life of Riley.

RULE 4:
Avoid "all-or-nothing" thinking

Recently at *Triathlon* magazine we received a manuscript entitled, "Short, Timed Workouts" from Dr. Joseph McEvoy, the aquatics director and swimming coach at Dickinson College in Carlisle, Pennsylvania. It was based on material from his book, *Fitness Swimming—Lifetime Programs* (Princeton Book Company, New Jersey, 1984).

"When the pressures of coaching built up this past winter during the middle of our competitive season," he wrote, "I seriously considered taking a few months off from my usual three- or four-times-a-week fitness program. I knew that I wouldn't feel as well as when I swim, but I simply didn't have an hour or more several times a week to spend stretching, warming up, working out, cooling down, and showering."

McEvoy's solution was to develop very short swimming sessions in which *time, not distance*, was the variable. The workouts fell short of the minimum requirements established by doctors and exercise physiologists for cardiovascular improvement, but they saved him from the ready-to-jump-out-of-my-skin withdrawal that consumes athletes who go off their sport cold turkey.

The creativity he drummed up in designing these short workouts served him in good stead when he returned to his usual regimen. "We think of exercise in 'all-or-nothing' terms," he continued. "Either we are on a full-scale training program, or we don't exercise at all. Perhaps a reduced-duration program, such as these 10- to 20-minute swimming workouts, can be a viable new option for you at times in your personal fitness program."

One Sample Workout

1 minute—easy swim
3 minutes—pull crawl (right arm only, keeping left arm extended in front for one length; left arm takes "return length," and so on)
3 minutes—kick with fins, crawl stroke
3 minutes—swim crawl
1 minute—easy swim
11 minutes total

Rest 1 minute between sets if necessary.

Monitor your heart rate carefully to ensure that you are working within your target heart range (see the figure on page 68).

We found McEvoy's stopgap remedy an honest, clear-thinking approach to the busy way we live. Short, timed sessions can be invaluable modular components when you're snowed under by other obligations. They may also serve as tune-ups for a sport you want to leave on the back burner for a while.

RULE 5:
Remember the rules of sports specificity

The starting gun blasted at the 1983 U.S. Triathlon Series race in Chicago, sending hundreds of triathletes plunging off the pier.

Moments later, series founder Carl Thomas, exhausted from his recent days of attending to last-minute details, thought he was hallucinating. "I glanced into the water and noticed some men paddling around right at the starting line, not going anywhere. I'd never seen anyone swim *vertically* before."

"A few burly types" were quickly fished out. None of them, it turned out, had ever swum a stroke in their lives. But they figured that since they were strong enough to run for miles, they could fake a mere mile in the water.

It's an extreme case—most people aren't quite whimsical enough to risk drowning—but it serves as a reminder that the only way to improve in a given sport is *by practicing that sport*. "Getting in better condition as a runner won't come anywhere near making you into a swimmer," warns John Duncan at the Cooper Clinic. The better you want to become as a cyclist, the more you must cycle. The better a triathlete you want to be, the more you must shore up your weakest sports.

If you heartily dislike a certain sport, recognize that your distaste may stem from insecurity. "Remind yourself that the improvement possibilities in triathloning are incredible," says multisport athlete Charlie Graves. "In some areas you've got no place to go but up, and that's what makes cross-training exciting. Work with someone who'll help you improve so fast that you'll get hooked."

"I was always looking for an excuse to skip my weak sports and slip out for a comfortable run instead," admits Sally Edwards. "Sometimes you have to counterattack with creativity. Invite a friend to participate, ride your bicycle to your favorite restaurant, swim in a different pool, or go to a fun run or race. When you begin to enjoy your weak sport more you'll avoid it less."

Don't underestimate how much strength your weak sports will sap out of you, especially at first. If you're a runner, a half-hour swim lesson will mow you flatter than a one-hour run at a fair clip. You're giving your body the message that new challenges are in store, and the newly bludgeoned response systems are serving notice that they're not entirely sure they like the idea. It will take a while for them to get used to it. Go slowly at first, be patient, and always warm up before a session and cool down afterward.

Torture, however, never earns extra merit points. If after repeated tries a certain sport truly fills you with fear and loathing, bid it adieu. One runner I know learned to love cycling but couldn't bring herself to stomach swimming. Instead, she bought a rowing machine because she was determined to get in some upper-body work, and she supplemented her routine with upper-body strength training. She won't be able to enter a traditional triathlon, but that was never her burning goal.

RULE 6:
Progress at your own rate: Aim for consistency

"When I first started running, I couldn't even get around the block," says Millie Brown. "In fact, it took a whole year before I was able to run a mile. But I figured my life was tough enough without making running a new hardship."

Brown ended up a study in accomplishment, because three years later she completed her first marathon. Her rate of progress doesn't even seem so slow in retrospect—three years is a relatively short time to jump from no running to racing 26 miles. "Consistency is the secret," advises middle-distance champion Linda Buchanan of Davis, California. "It's the sure key to success."

The consistency required for someone like Brown, over 40 and with no athletic background, to achieve the same endurance level in cycling and swimming attracted the ABC-TV cameras when she entered her second Ironman in 1983. As the TV van filmed her on the cycling course and photographers draped themselves out of car windows to snap shots, a cyclist darting past yelled back, "Hey! What's going on? You famous or something?"

"No!" she said. "They're filming me because I'm not!"

RULE 7:
Don't forget strength training and stretching

Strength
Many triathletes concentrating on endurance work feel that weight lifting is a diversion that risks adding too much muscle. It's true that lifting heavy weights can rob a runner of litheness, but strength work has changed since the days of dank gyms. If you want more power, definition, or a head start in developing the muscles you'll need in a new sport, don't rely on aerobics alone.

Use strength work to prepare muscles for unfamiliar aerobic

demands, but only under the direction of a knowledgeable coach or exercise physiologist who can save you time by demonstrating the correct way to lift to build the muscle mass you want. If you're a puny-legged swimmer, strengthen the offending sectors before you hit the road. If you're a runner or cyclist with scant upper-body definition, some prescribed curls, lateral raises, and pull-downs can save you time as you tackle swimming. If you bulk up in a way that seriously affects your performance, ease back on your lifting.

Stretching

Flexibility work is one of those things, like flossing, we know we'd be better off doing but never quite get around to. For starters, stretching is *not* the same as warming up. Warming-up implies very slowly going through the motions of the actual exercise. If your muscles are cold, hard stretching will subject them to microscopic tears and snaps somewhat like pulling saltwater taffy just removed from the refrigerator. Warm up your muscles before you stretch. Stretching can then be a psychologically calming, centering routine that will help you adjust to the demanding exercise ahead.

Bob Anderson, known as the "stretching guru" to countless professional athletes, including the Denver Broncos, developed a streamlined stretching program specifically for this book and for cross-trainers who plan to concentrate on endurance work.

Flexibility for novice triathletes
by Bob Anderson

Stretching will make the triathlete's transition from one activity to another much easier. When done with personal sensitivity, relaxation, and control, stretching will reduce or eliminate excess muscle tension or tightness, prevent or reduce muscle soreness, and maintain or increase current flexibility levels—benefits that a triathlete can really appreciate.

Stretching allows you at least to maintain your present flexibility, while offsetting the gradual loss of muscle elasticity often associated with running and cycling. It should also have a positive effect on muscular endurance by allowing you to feel limber for a longer period of time. Stretching will make it easier for the triathlete to adapt to the flexibility demanded in swimming.

Overstretching is the biggest mistake people make. If you stretch too far, you actually cause the contraction of the muscles being stretched. When this reflex is activated, proper stretching is impossible. Pain and the inability to relax are indications that you are overstretching, which is useless and potentially harmful.

Stretching should be done slowly, without bouncing. Your stretch should feel slight and easy. Hold this for 5–30 seconds. As you hold it, the feeling of tension should diminish. If it doesn't, ease off a little into a more comfortable stretch. The easy stretch reduces tension and readies the tissues for the developmental stretch.

After holding the easy stretch, move a fraction of an inch farther into it until you feel mild tension again. Hold this *developmental stretch* for 5–30 seconds. This feeling should also slightly diminish or remain the same. If the pull in your muscles increases or becomes painful, you are overstretching. Ease off a bit to a comfortable stretch. This stage reduces muscle tension and will safely increase flexibility.

Hold only stretches that feel good to you. The key to stretching is to be relaxed as you concentrate on the area being worked. Your breathing should be slow, deep, and rhythmic. Don't worry about how far you can stretch. Be relaxed, and limberness will be one of the many by-products of regular stretching.

Stretch both before and after activity when possible. In any event, stretch at least 20–40 minutes every 24 hours. Get into the habit of stretching two or three times during the day for several minutes, and for 10–20 minutes before going to sleep.

Before competition, spend more time stretching the

muscles that tend to get stiff or tired during a race. It is important to do the stretches that you find the most helpful. With experience, you will develop a sequence of stretches that will best fit your individual needs—and will add creativity and variety to your program.

Get into the habit of massaging your feet and elevating them every day. This will help keep your legs, feet, and back always feeling good and ready to go.

Massaging Feet

With your thumbs, massage up and down the longitudinal arch of your foot. Use circular motions with a good amount of pressure to loosen tissues. Do both feet. Always massage your feet for 2–3 minutes before and after activity or after sitting or standing for long periods of time. This will reduce unwanted tension and keep the feet and legs feeling good.

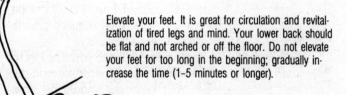

Elevate your feet. It is great for circulation and revitalization of tired legs and mind. Your lower back should be flat and not arched or off the floor. Do not elevate your feet for too long in the beginning; gradually increase the time (1–5 minutes or longer).

Streamlined stretching guides are included in the chapters on swimming, cycling, running, and race day (Chapters 4–6, 9).

ILLUSTRATIONS BY JEAN ANDERSON. STRETCHES EXCERPTED FROM *TRIATHLETE STRETCHES* CHART (22½ x 33", $4 POSTPAID) © 1984 AND THE BOOK *STRETCHING* BY BOB ANDERSON © 1980. STRETCHING INC., P.O. BOX 767, PALMER LAKE, CO 80133.

Refine technique by building a mileage foundation

Once you have learned new techniques and exercise systems, you can:

1. Build an endurance stress base.
2. Further address the biomechanical differences in each sport until they "run together" so that you feel involved in *one* training system to effect total conditioning, not three.
3. Develop the physical and mental acumen required over long distances.
4. Begin training your body to use its fat stores for energy in the latter parts of long-distance work.

Some definitions

Aerobic: Literally, "with oxygen." All of your body fuels need oxygen in order to burn metabolically. Aerobic work means that you are supplying all systems with enough oxygen to be consumed, transported, and used at a steady rate. Your cardiovascular and respiratory systems will improve their ability to supply your muscles with oxygen as they adapt to the higher demands placed on them in training. As your oxygen-delivery systems improve and the ability of the active muscles to use the supplied oxygen increases, your fitness level improves.

"Aerobics" encompasses activities that emphasize endurance work as opposed to all-out bursts of energy. Swimming, cycling, running, and triathloning are aerobic; sprinting and weight lifting are not.

Physiologists agree that aerobic training done at approximately 65–75% of your maximum heart rate (see "How to Compute Your Training Intensity," page 68) for at least 12–20 minutes three times a week is the threadbare minimum to maintain–but not improve– cardiovascular fitness. Five or six sessions of 30–60 minutes per week are needed to upgrade your present level.

The target numbers slide around somewhat, depending on the source. Skilled athletes with fast, refined recovery rates consider 80% of maximum the requisite upper limit for aerobic work, while others caution that 50% is sufficient for unathletic or older people. The Karvonen method, as detailed in a study by M. K.

Kentala and O. Mustala in 1957 in *The Effects of Training Heart Rate*: A *Longitudinal Study*, designates 60–90% as the sliding range (with 65–75% as the average beginning athlete's usual target range for aerobic work).

To give yourself a sense of the way aerobic work feels, some athletes advise sprinting and then dropping right below that level and maintaining it for your designated exercise time. Venerable James E. ("Doc") Counsilman, Ph.D., of Indiana University, (Mark Spitz's swimming coach, as well as the driving force behind the 1972 and 1976 men's Olympic teams) says, "Try the talking test. If someone stops you at the end of the pool and you can't answer a question because you're gasping, then you're working too hard."

Long, Slow Distance. Known—who says these folks don't have a sense of humor?—as LSD. This is relatively self-explanatory, describing aerobic work done at a steady rate for an extended time over a long distance. Endorphins, the body's morphinelike natural painkillers, kick in during such exercise and result in what's called "runner's euphoria," or the ebullient equivalent in other sports as well.

Over-distance training. A variation of LSD. It implies training a longer distance than you intend to complete in a race, but at less than racing speed, for the purpose of concentrating on stroke mechanics, pacing, and cardiovascular upkeep.

1. Determine how hard your heart works when you're at rest by taking your pulse for 10 seconds and multiplying it by 6. Your resting pulse rate (RPR) is best computed in the morning soon after rising but before significant activity.

2. The number 220 shown below signifies a theoretical maximum heart rate that is typically reduced by one beat per minute for each year you age. If you've had your maximum heart rate (MHR) computed through personal testing, use that number instead of 220. Simply multiply by 65–75% and then add your RPR to get your target working range.

3. Every reference source gives a different percentage range for aerobic work. The Karvonen method puts it at 60–90 of maximum, with lower-intensity, longer-duration exercise for inexperienced athletes and higher-intensity, shorter-duration work for

those in strong cardiovascular condition. Generally speaking, 65–75 is a good starting place if you're beginning cross-training. Your amount of recovery time will help you determine if you're working too hard or not hard enough.

4. After a while you will know instinctively how it feels to push your body at its proper aerobic level, and you needn't be a slave to the clock.

Pulse Rates: How to Compute Your Target Training Intensity

	The Formula		Example	
	220		220	
	− your age		− 32	(Brad's age)
			188	
	− your resting pulse		− 60	
	rate (RPR)		128	128
for low end	× 65%		× .65	× .75
& high end			83.2	96
of target	+ RPR		+ 60	+ 60
range			143.2	156

Divide both results by 6 to facilitate	÷ 6	
10-second counts per minute	23.86	26

Maximum heart rate (MHR) for beginning aerobics

24–26 pulse beats per 10 seconds for target range of 65–75%

1. Take your pulse immediately after exercise for *10 seconds.* In Brad's case, it should be 24–26 beats.

2. More highly conditioned athletes should determine formulas in a slightly higher range.

3. Recheck your RPR every so often. As you become more conditioned, your pulse rate will drop.

5. Check your pulse every now and then during exercise to see that you're working in the target range.

You must establish a solid foundation of aerobic work in each sport—meaning many miles of learning technique through long, slow distance—before you can proceed. That may take any-

---

Measuring Aerobic Improvement

Example

1. Rest 2 minutes after strenuous, continuous exercise in high end of target range.

1. After running 4 miles, Brad rested 2 minutes and

2. Count your pulse beats for 10 seconds and multiply by 6.

2. counted 18 pulse beats in 10 seconds $\times 6 =$

3. If your pulse exceeds 130 beats per minute (bpm), you may be working too hard.

3. bpm of 108.

4. The Karvonen method suggests that a 10-second count of less than 20 (120 bpm) is desirable.

4. Count was less than 20, as recommended.

5. Keep track of your recovery rates. As your fitness level improves, so will your capacity to work at a higher aerobic intensity.

To make adjustments on your target range, keep close tabs on your recovery rate. That's the time it takes for your heart to drop back to its resting level after exercise. This happens *faster*—meaning that the numbers *decrease*—the more fit you become. Top athletes can have resting pulse rates in the high-40s to mid-50s, meaning that they have such good cardiovascular efficiency that their hearts are taking fewer but stronger beats, with more rest in between each beat and more blood pumped each time. As your fitness level improves, you will notice a gradual decline in your morning's resting pulse rate. If it increases, you may be working too hard—meaning that you're not giving your heart enough chance to rest and recover between workouts.

where from six to eight weeks to a year or more, as in Millie Brown's case, depending on your skill level and the time you invest.

Keep track of your progress by jotting down in your training diary not only the number of miles, but also how you are feeling. "You're doing this to feel better. Make it a hobby," says Charlie Graves. "The whole point at this stage is to make the learning process fun, not go after monster mileage. Take as many weeks or months as you need. Be consistent, and it'll happen in no time."

RULE 8:
Think time, not distance

Begin cross-training right away with some revolutionary thinking. Although the emphasis now is on establishing a mileage base, *don't* set goal distances per week, and never make up for a missed session by doubling your workout the next day. Instead, allot a certain number of *hours* per week that you will devote to triathlon-ing, and make adjustments as you go along. See how far you can go during that time, *making certain that you work within the proper 65–75% aerobic speed* (or slightly higher, if you're a well-conditioned and experienced athlete) to avoid undertraining and to accustom yourself to focusing on intensity, even when it's slow and steady. How all of this is changing you is more important than how far you go. "You're going easy now," says Bob Curtis, "but that doesn't mean you have time for garbage mileage."

"Let's say you decide to run 15 miles a week for your first month," says Julie Moss. "You might end up with impressive mileage totals, but they say nothing about the shape you're in. How long did it take you? Were you running too fast or too slowly?"

"Don't think, 'Since I ran a mile yesterday, I'll try two today,'" says Dave Scott. "Think of running 20 minutes instead of the 15 you managed the week before. To maximize your efforts given time constraints, emphasize the right *intensity*, not covering a certain number of miles."

Besides, cross-training will irrevocably muddle your ideas about the value of mile numbers. Two miles in the pool is a substantial over-distance session, 2 miles of cycling a mere warm-up, no matter what your athletic background is. Although 5 miles of running is said to equal 1 of swimming (based on the fact that world-class swimmers can cover 200 meters in 100 seconds, while their running counterparts cover that distance in about 20), what happens when running and swimming are done consecutively? What are the compounded values of the supposedly equitable distances?

Veteran ocean swimmer Harald Johnson, 35, gave a demonstration of how this time game works to dramatic effect as he prepared for his 28.5-mile Swim Around Manhattan in 1983. Although a perennial competitor, he had never raced even half that far before. Instead of repeatedly testing if he could "go the distance," he let his waterproof watch take over. His longest training session in the months before the swim was only 3 hours—an incredibly long submersion, but less than one-third the time it would take the winner to circumnavigate New York.

"That was all I needed to know I could do it," explained Johnson after winning the race in just over 8 hours. "Going into it already knowing how much 28 miles was going to hurt would have made me hold back. I needed that element of surprise to make New York special. It would have ruined the sense of adventure that was leading me there in the first place if I'd done a 28-miler before the race. Besides, running marathoners don't train for a big event by putting in 26 miles over and over beforehand. All training amounts to is reaching that moment when your mind tells you that you're ready."

Although he was in top condition before training for the race and already knew exactly how he sized up against many of his competitors, Johnson's use of time instead of racking up megamileage still works for beginning cross-trainers. I certainly could have used it years ago as I trained for a 2-mile postal-event swim (self-timed races in which you mail in your results) by cranking out 2 miles every day for weeks before race time to make sure I could manage it. I could do it, all right, but was so enervated from overkill that I finished with a disappointing and lackluster 20 seconds to spare before the 1-hour cutoff time.

Using time to devise a fitness schedule.
1K swim, 30K bike, 10K run (½, 20, 6 miles) = goal distances

Sample week: January
(for a runner just learning to swim)

	Monday	Tuesday	Wednesday	Thursday	Friday	Saturday	Sunday
Swim	7:30 P.M. swimming lesson		7:30 P.M. swimming lesson		7:30 P.M. swimming lesson		Rest
Bike		45-minute ride		45-minute ride			
Run	45-minute run, some hills		1-hour easy run			½-hour run	

Total hours: 3 hours swimming/techniques
1½ hours cycling/LSD/work on smoother gearing
2¼ hours running/easy aerobics
6¾ hours exercising

Comments: 1. Lifted head up too far to breathe in swimming.
2. Ran better after warming up and stretching—add more flexibility work.
3. Learn to repair tires!
4. In two weeks try increasing 10% (running and cycling only) = 7 hours, 10 minutes, more or less.

Johnson's aquatic instincts and inductive arrival at the moment of recognition came through experience, and the less skilled you are the less thrilled you should be by what he calls the element of surprise: Eventually your aim is to hit precisely such a peak of creative guessing that endurance work is pushed entirely into that virtuoso realm of mental conditioning and control.

RULE 9:
Reaching your aerobic plateau

Although your rate of progress is unconditionally an individual matter, a common rule of thumb is to increase your training time by no more than 10 percent per week (see formula, below) in any one sport. If you wish ultimately to spend only an hour per day in training, cut back at first to make allowances for the unfamiliar stresses of new disciplines. If you suffer overtraining effects at any time (see Rule 10), cut your workload back before attempting another 10 percent increase.

"Plan a 6-hour fitness week and see how many multiples of your goal distance you can do," suggests triathlete Dean Harper. "Balance it and mix everything up for variety."

Continue these 10 percent increments until the distances you are doing each equal either *three times* what you plan to attempt in a race or, for noncompetitors, three times your goal distances. Since Brad Munson's goal is to swim ½ mile, cycle 20, and run 6, his aerobic plateau would mean working up to 1½ miles of swimming, 60 of cycling, and 18 of running per week. Brad's chart ("Three times the goal distances = plateau phase") shows how he let time tell him when he was ready.

Formula for strengthening the aerobic base

(Time spent per activity) × (10 percent) = weekly increase of time.

When (weekly distance) = (3 × goal distances or race distances) = aerobic base established.

When aerobic base established = plateau phase.

Maintain plateau phase at this time level for a minimum of 6–8 weeks. Aim for consistency and let your skill level dictate the length of this phase.

Should overtraining symptoms occur at any phase, add more rest days

Three times the goal distances = plateau phase   Sample week: April

	Monday	Tuesday	Wednesday	Thursday	Friday	Saturday	Sunday
Swim	½-hour lap swimming (¾ mile)		½-hour lap swimming + kick sets		Day off		1-hour swim: broken mile + kick sets
Bike		45-minute cycle to work; 1-hour cycle home followed by:				2-hour ride with friends (scenic route)	
Run		15-minute easy run off bicycle		15-mile run			

Total hours: 8 hours, 20 minutes of exercising

Distances: 2½ swimming, 17 running, 60 cycling (miles)

3 × goal distances should equal = 1½ swimming, 18 running, 60 cycling (miles)

Comments: 1. Heart range 70-75% of maximum capacity.
2. Trying to do more swimming; getting ready to add intervals. Cut back on running.
3. Rest day scheduled after long run.
4. Longer and fewer LSD sessions—long rides up the coast are perfect!
5. Would like to hold this plateau phase about four months.

to your schedule and cut back on training intensity before proceeding to the next level.

Use the plateau phase to sharpen your skills and acclimate yourself to long endurance work.

After this phase, you will maintain the same amount of training time by reducing time and mileage to accommodate sessions of higher-quality work.

Discover new cross-training gears

The next step in making the most of your training time involves:

1. Changing the emphasis to higher-quality workouts by adding new speed "gears" to your repertoire.

2. Budgeting cross-training even more astutely into your schedule and raising performance levels by balancing interval work with complete rest.

3. Note: No sugar coating here. We are now discussing pain. This accelerated level requires a high athletic aptitude and is more exhausting per second than LSD because it exerts more forceful demands on your heart.

Maimonides, a twelfth-century Spanish philosopher, advocated exercise to the point of breathlessness. In the evolution of many species, survival has often depended on sudden violent effort rather than an even-keel approach. This ingrained pattern continues, despite the pacifying buffers of technology.

First, to understand whence this need for violent effort springs, let's review the general (or stress) adaptation principle. It holds that an organism, muscle, or enzyme system stressed beyond its threshold will recover *slightly beyond that level* if allowed time to rebuild and repair itself. *Overload work* is what the phrase implies. You are stressing your body just beyond what it can handle (called *demand*), essentially breaking the systems down.

The systems will, however, rise to the occasion and reconstruct themselves to the level you insisted on *if allowed adequate rest time*. If this rest time is either too short or nonexistent, an added overload session on the same systems will only break them down further. When David Costill describes the body adapting to *properly managed* stress for amazing improvement, this is exactly what he means.

If you're swimming or cycling or running the same distance every day, you are making less of a demand than your body has already accommodated itself to—which explains why your mono-chromatic routine is actually more dismal than ever or why you consequently feel the need to annex more and more miles to compensate for your diminishing returns.

This phenomenon is comparable to the *set-point theory* that drives dieters crazy. The body, well-padded though it may be, will grow accustomed to a certain number of calories per day and will interpret reduced intake as a threat of starvation. It will first issue gnawing hunger pains in protest, and then, much the way a bear hibernates, it will protect itself by slowing down the rate of metabolism, stubbornly burning only the number of calories it receives. That's why even if you stick to your diet, you hit a seemingly endless plateau during which you don't see any im-provement.

After the body gets used to the idea of dieting—as if it needed time to adjust to the infliction of a new training system—the survival fear dissipates and the body presses its stored fuels into service.

How it works

To understand how high-quality exercise—also called "intermit-tent exercise," "interval training," or "dash training"—works, some experiments by famed Swedish exercise physiologist Per Olof-Astrand may help. He is generally credited with popularizing interval training by discovering in the early 1960s that when exercise was divided into short periods (30–60 seconds each) of work and rest, it was easier to continue the exercise, thereby improving endurance capacity, for a longer period of time.

Using this short-work/short-rest formula, tests showed that cir-culatory and respiratory systems produced *the same results* as continuous submaximal work (meaning longer-lasting, lower-intensity aerobics). When the alternating work and rest periods were increased to 2–3 minutes each, however, the physiological responses were closer to those expected during hard, continuous exercise that soon ends in fatigue. In other words, short work and short rest paradoxically allow a higher performance for a longer time than hard effort followed by a long rest in which the heart rate drops and is then yanked back up to sprinting speed.

The physical mechanisms that might explain why this works aren't completely clear. One hypothesis is that the myoglobin contained in the muscles may act as a storage depot for oxygen. Aerobic exercise can be performed until these oxygen stores are depleted. Brief recovery periods then allow these stores to be replenished with oxygen from the blood. When the periods of work and rest are lengthened, however, as in the 2–3-minute formula, there might not be enough oxygen in the blood to replenish the supply adequately to maintain aerobic conditions, and exhaustion sets in.

Energetics, by Clarence M. Agress, M.D. (Grosset & Dunlap, 1978), reported a related study by Ralph S. Paffenbarger and Wayne E. Hale of the California State Department of Health and the University of California School of Public Health, illustrating how a system of hard work plus complete rest, instead of steady, lower-level work, yields the best results in the shortest time. Paffenbarger and Hale examined the mortality rates of 6351 San Francisco longshoremen, generally sedentary off the job, over a 22-year period. During work, their cargo loading was classified as having heavy-, moderate- or light-energy output.

The heavy workers had many repeated periods of hard labor interspersed with rest at a steady pace (55 percent of their time was spent working and 45 at rest). The mortality rate for this group was 26.9 per 10,000 work-years, compared to 46 and 49 for the other groups. Even more amazing was that the sudden death rate of the high-activity group was less than one-third that of the low-activity group.

This study points to stress plus rest as the best life-insurance policy. Maintaining a constant moderate work load, concluded the researchers and Agress, offered less protection against heart attack than shorter-duration, higher-intensity work.

Some definitions

Anaerobic. Literally, "without oxygen." When the intensity of exercise is so high that the body can no longer function aerobically, you cross the **anaerobic threshold** and near exhaustion quickly. Sprinting at over 75–85% of your maximum heart rate is anaerobic work and can be maintained for only short, intense periods.

Lactic acid is the end product of anaerobic metabolism. The anaerobic threshold is reached when the rate of lactic acid diffusion into the bloodstream exceeds its rate of removal from the blood.

Anaerobic threshold is a relatively new concept and there isn't a world of data about training to improve it. Note: Evidence suggests that any work load that causes excess lactate to accumulate provides a stimulus for aerobic improvement, because the body's ability to tolerate lactic acid is improved though training. In other words, the higher the level of lactate and the longer the time you can tolerate it, the longer you will be able to endure when the going gets tough. The trick is to develop your anaerobic systems through interval training so that your body makes increasingly efficient recoveries from high lactate infusions, and thereby learns to function longer with the product of hard work in its system.

Fartlek. Swedish for "speedplay." It involves mixing paces and, technically, using slopes to vary the amount of effort. This is like cross-country running—enjoying the scenery along the way. Using this "gear" keeps your stomach, shoulder, and other muscles from tightening in the fixed pace of a standard run and adds variety to your exercise.

High-quality sets. A group of repeats performed at an intensity level greater than that of any other set in the workout. Its intensity is close to the pace used during a race.

Intervals. Training in segments—intervals—according to the clock. You may affix a set amount of rest time after each segment, or, for higher-quality work, the rest time is determined by subtracting the effort time from the total preordained interval time. For instance, suppose you are swimming a set of ten 100-yard sprints with a designated interval time of 1:30. If you complete one of those sprints in 1:20, you have 10 seconds to rest before the next "send-off" time is up.

Killer repeats. What Scott Tinley calls 1-minute fast, 1-minute slow—done ad infinitum on a bicycle (cf. fartlek training).

Negative splitting. Performing the second half of a designated distance or set faster than the first.

Repeats, or repetition training. In preparation for a particular event, repeats involve shorter distances and greater speeds than in a race. The rest interval allows an almost complete recovery of the heart and respiratory rate (cf. striders).

Striders. A common training technique among pro football players in which 110-yard dashes are broken by long rest. The heart rate is allowed to drop to around 120 beats per minute (bpm) before the next strider. Requiring the heart to jump back up to a much higher level is particularly grueling.

Tapering. A crucial resting period when the training load is decreased in preparation for a race. The length of tapering depends on the event, the training intensity, and the individual. I should have used this theory when gearing up for my 2-mile postal-event swim.

VO_2 max. Maximal oxygen consumption or uptake. Improving your oxygen consumption capabilities increases your heart's stroke volume (amount of blood pumped per beat), cardiac output, blood flow and volume, capillary mass, and density and muscular adaptation to intense work.

New studies show that the percentage of time you can maintain a high level is a better determinant of aerobic efficiency than the top percentage you can hit at any one time.

To illustrate how intense anaerobic work accelerates aerobic improvement, let's say your friend has entrusted you with his brand new car. You'd like the ride to be smooth and steady, preferably with both you and the car escaping injury. You still

Three Training Styles: Aerobic, Anaerobic, VO₂ Max

Training System	Target Heart Ranges				
	Recovering Cardiac Patient (Elderly)	Average-Fitness Athlete		Highly Conditioned Athlete	
Aerobic	50–60	65–75		70–80	
		Beginners	More advanced	Less experienced	More experienced
Anaerobic		After aerobic plateau established			
		70–80		75–85	
		Non-competitor	More advanced, potential competitor	Less experienced	More experienced
VO₂ Max				80–90*	
				*Very intense: recommend doctor's consent	

need the wherewithal to shift into high cruising speed, move with quick bursts, and occasionally floor it—not because it's more thrilling that way, but because safe driving often depends on such quick responses. The sum total is skilled, even-tempered driving.

Your cross-training transmission, with its emphasis on conserving time and developing all possible systems for overall condi-

Description	Example (Swimming)	Purpose
Long, slow distance work—can be maintained from 20 minutes to several hours	Comfortable, continuous-effort mile	Improve stroke, mechanics, develop rhythm, learn a sense of pacing
Cannot be maintained indefinitely; short efforts and short rest or long efforts and short rest	9 × 150-yard intervals with short rest—heart rate drops only 10–15% during rest	Trains one to compete at maximum aerobic level; elevates blood lactate levels; improves the ability of muscles to extract oxygen from the blood
Long efforts and long rests*	6 × 300-yard repeats—heart rate allowed to recover 30–40% (for example, 1½ minutes of rest after 3–10 minutes of effort)	Improves maximal oxygen consumption

tioning, works exactly the same way. Smooth racing sometimes requires flooring it.

Dr. Kenneth Cooper gives a clear example of why athletes must combine anaerobic training with aerobic work. Until the aerobics era burst on us in the late 1960s, coaches instructed their football players to concentrate on sprinting and muscle building. After all,

Emphasizing individual workouts
Longer and Fewer Long, Slow Distance Sessions and Stress + Rest

Sample week: July

	Monday	Tuesday	Wednesday	Thursday	Friday	Saturday	Sunday
Swim	45-minute timed mile + kick and pull sets		¾-hour fitness class—adding intervals		Rest		Rest
Bike		1 minute on/ 1 minute off (easy) × 20				45 minutes cycling, easy pace practicing corners, followed by:	
Run				12-mile easy jog		slow 1-mile run	

Comments: 1. Longer but fewer runs.
2. First interval work in pool and in cycling.
3. Tired on Sunday. Played softball and went to museums.
4. Goal: Buy a wind-load simulator. Not spending as much time cycling as I'd like.

their game depended on sheer brawn and quick sprints from the line. The players were strong and had trained themselves for fast running at short distances, but their energy dwindled drastically during the second half, and the incidence of injuries became higher toward the end of the game. The players lacked the endurance training necessary to continue.

Conversely, unless you train your anaerobic systems, you aren't giving yourself any race-ready gears. Distance athletes must develop anaerobic capacities in case they must turn on the juice during a race, and likewise sprinters need the stamina to finish a race at maximum speed.

You're now ready to concentrate on individual workouts, shifting the emphasis even more from weekly mileage totals. LSD sessions become longer but fewer. A 15-mile run once a week will yield better endurance results than four 6-milers in the same time. You're putting in far less time and almost half the distance, but the greater over-distance intensity and stamina required in that 15-mile session better resembles the long-endurance work you're training for.

Maintain this interval schedule a minimum of 6–8 weeks, and then taper before your race or a timed session of your goal distances.

RULE 10:
Avoiding overtraining and sports addiction

> More men are killed by overwork than the importance of
> the world justifies
>
> —Rudyard Kipling

It's a tall order to convince a 35-year-old businessperson who demands quick returns on an investment that rest is as important to getting ahead as work. If you spend upwards of $500 on a bicycle, you probably are anxious to see results fast, and that could mean overtraining problems.

Ask yourself the following questions.

1. Does physical fitness seem like another stress in my life?
2. Am I anxious and emotionally spent after a workout?
3. Am I restless or sleeping too many hours?

4. Do I often feel tired, rundown, or listless?

5. Am I short-tempered with family, friends, or co-workers?

6. Does work or my family suddenly seem to be making unreasonable demands on my time?

7. Am I frustrated by lack of progress in my training?

8. Do I feel rudderless and easily upset?

If you answered yes to any of those questions, you are ruining all your efforts by overtraining. Don't underestimate the impact emotional stress will have on your physical abilities, and if your head doesn't stop falling in the soup at dinner, you will be out of a big investment because your family will dismantle your bicycle unless you stop being a slave to your endorphins.

"If you start experiencing such overuse injuries as minor irritation or inflammations, sleepiness, irritable reactions to situations, general personality changes, or an elevated heart rate while resting, you're not pacing your training correctly," says John Kovaleski at Costill's lab. "The important thing is pacing yourself over an entire competitive year, not crowding quality work all into a short time."

"People who overtrain run a greater risk of developing coronary disease," confirms John Duncan at the Cooper Clinic.

If you're a novice triathlete, observing the following will guard against overtraining.

1. Never do interval work in the same sport on consecutive days.

2. Never do more than one interval session in each sport per week. (More highly conditioned athletes can accommodate more interval training.)

3. Assess the different recovery rates of each sport when planning rests. Weigh the effects of each sport's environment. Swimming will cool and regulate your body temperature, facilitating heat dissipation and a faster recovery time. Wind will cool a cyclist better than it will a runner.

If you're a cyclist, running may seem less foreign than swimming, but the impact trauma on a hot summer day during a 2-mile run will exact a greater toll than swimming half the distance in a temperature-regulated pool. Allow more recovery time for running on both a daily and a long-term basis. You're making your heart work harder because you're in a vertical position, and you're moving a much larger muscle mass than when you're swimming or even cycling.

4. Use all the different speed methods at your disposal to add variety to your training. It's much easier to psych yourself up for a round of hill running knowing that the reward is either a day of rest or an easy cycling ride the following day. Going into each workout of the same distance with a vague sense of "pushing as hard as I can" is exactly where the "automatic drive" sensation descends. Interval days are anticipated for their brevity, and LSD days are a welcome relief from intensity.

It's better to take planned rests than to suffer injury (often the result of muscles not allowed sufficient repair time), forcing you to lay off for longer than you would otherwise. Some triathletes even try to apply elaborate biorhythm principles to designing their programs by keeping close tabs on their feelings during exercise to see if they can predict those mysterious "off days" we all have occasionally. They then try to plot their training so that intense workouts fall only on strong days.

Here's a guide to detecting and preventing overtraining.

1. Monitor your morning pulse rate a few moments after rising but prior to any substantial exertion; note any sudden changes.

2. Keep track of any sudden or drastic weight loss or gain. If you are losing weight too rapidly, raid the refrigerator and skip a day of training.

3. Always keep watch on your heart rate to ensure that you are working at proper and safe levels.

4. Warm up before a session and cool down afterward, particularly during interval training.

5. Take whole days off, at least one or two per week, as a reward for your progress.

6. Get plenty of rest and avoid alcohol for at least several hours after exercise.

7. Drink as much water as you can stand before, during, and after exercise.

8. When in doubt, rest.

Finally, remember that psychologists warn us that we must

reward ourselves when we accomplish a goal, no matter how incidental it seems, or we are doomed to keep repeating the same feat at the same level forever. Celebrate every success, even the small ones, before you move on.

Cross-training = the sum of speed and technque gears

Now that you are focusing more on each individual workout,

1. Combine sports in a single workout to assimilate the biomechanical and muscular benefits of transitions.

2. Assemble training sessions by choosing from a variety of slow to fast speeds and all possible techniques.

3. Learn how to pace combined-sport efforts so that you cross-peak over a long-endurance bout—the final goal of cross-training.

Thinking as a cross-trainer means constructing workouts that combine what could be described as modular blocks of all the different speeds and techniques now open to you.

If you run 4 miles to your half-hour swimming lesson in which you focus on high elbow recovery during long-interval sets, for example, you are combining a lower-body LSD block with an upper-body interval-and-technique block. The entire two-sport session need only take an hour. But the pacing and muscular transitions required in that cross-training run mean that you are no longer simply a runner. They mark the end of thinking as a single-sport specialist and the beginning of thinking as a triathlete.

At this stage, a 20-mile ride immediately followed by a 5-mile run can have the same training effect as a 20-mile ride and 10-mile run separated by several hours. With the first plan, fewer hours are spent, there's less potential for impact trauma injuries in running, and you're teaching your body how to adjust to muscular transitions.

Settling into a consecutive sport will take a few moments of adjustment. "Always run after you get off your bike," recommends triathlete Bill Ruth of Bethlehem, Pennsylvania. Robert Patton of Los Angeles, a two-time Ironman finisher, arranges his 50-hour workweek so that he can run from his office to the YMCA swimming pool for an hour workout at lunchtime two days a week. The swimming stretches his legs out after the run, and he has time to shower and get back to his desk within 2 hours. Linda Buchanan, on the other hand, likes to swim before continued aerobic work with another sport. "I prefer stretching out first," she says.

Combining sports allows you to graft fitness onto your day at times when it seems that there's no time to exercise. Since you are no longer bound by that 6 P.M. swimming workout every day, cross-training creatively enters your social life. "Try cycling to a friend's house for dinner and arranging for a ride home afterward," says Mark Wendley, a triathlete who works a 40-hour week as a magazine accountant. "Or run to and from a Saturday matinee. Sound crazy? It is! But I'll bet you'll be able to find friends and family members willing to join you—at least partway."

RULE 11:
Learning the art of pacing

Pacing is a matter of putting it all together so that you know—at least more often than not—how fast you're parceling out your energy sources so that your combined sports efforts cross-peak. If you're in a triathlon, you want to manage your resources so that you cross the line exhausted but not devastated. Over-distance training and watching the clock will teach you pacing. Interval work will also help you understand how your body feels at high speed, and *how it feels to maintain that speed over a long distance*.

To test your pacing in gearing up to run a marathon, for example, you can use this formula.

1. Run a 10K race at maximum effort. You then know fairly well how far you can stress yourself.

2. Figure out your splits (the time it takes you to run each separate mile). You should be able to run a marathon at a 5 percent slower pace. If you run a 10K with an average of 7-minute splits, you should run a marathon at 7:25 per mile and be depleted right as you cross the finish line.

Learning triathloning and sports-combined pacing is a bit touchier. There are neither standard terrains nor fixed distances. That's a large part of triathloning's charm, but it turns any would-

Two-Sport Sessions and Practicing Transitions

Sample week: September

	Monday	Tuesday	Wednesday	Thursday	Friday	Saturday	Sunday
Swim	½-hour run to 1-hour swim, fitness-interval work, + ½-mile warm-up		1-hour swim, fitness class (intervals)		1-hour swim, fitness class (intervals)		Rest
Bike		30 minutes cycling; 20 min. LSD + 5 one-minute on/ off followed by				2-hour easy cycling fol- lowed by:	
Run		20-minute run		½-hour timed track intervals		20-minute run	

Time: Swimming: 3 hours, cycling: 2½ hours, running: 1 hour, 40 minutes
Total: 7 hours, 10 minutes
Comments: 1. Doing swim intervals at 80% of heart rate.
2. Tuesday hardest day! Swimming stretched out sore muscles next day.
3. Need longer runs next week.
4. Easy swim or cycling good "down time" on rest day—for fun more than exercise.

be pacing formulas into guesswork. Is it easier for a swimmer in a triathlon to pace herself later during the run because she's conserved energy in her strong event, or is the runner who's finishing off with her best segment, but cross-bonking from the swimming and cycling, in the best position?

For short triathlons that involve a 15K footrace at the end, Sally Edwards recommends trying to run at 90–95 percent of your fastest 10K pace, (for highly skilled runners only) and figure that it gets more complicated the longer the triathlon distance.

We are as near to heaven by sea as by land.
—Sir Humphrey Gilbert (1539–1583)

People loved telling me the horrors I'd run into ("They throw *bodies* in the East River, you jerk") when I swam around Manhattan. By the time I climbed in, I had this terrible image of flesh falling off bones everywhere, the way meat disintegrates off overcooked chicken.

Less than an hour into the race, I knew they were right. Something strange was bobbing in the distance. Suddenly I realized that I was swimming straight for a big patch of shrunken heads.

I detoured off, but as I drew alongside the heads I was stunned to see that they were very neatly collected in maybe a dozen mesh bags. I sprinted hard to get away. They registered as a blur, and only when I was in the clear did my brain flash the picture right. Someone had thrown bags of cantaloupes—a mélange of melons— into the river! I'd been scared by a field of fruit.

It snapped the fear out of me. After that, all I could feel was the city. When I swam beneath bridges they vibrated with cars. Even though it was a Sunday, I imagined in the morning that all those people were going to work, and toward the end of the day I listened to the cars going in the opposite direction and pretended that those were the same people going home now. Their day was over, but I was still at it.

That's what happens to you in the water. Your imagination ignites when you swim, and you feel connections, good and bad, that you can never discover any other way. I was told to expect the worst, swimming around New York. All I got was the best.

—Harald Johnson, 35,
Los Angeles
Magazine publisher

CHAPTER 4

Swimming: Inner pacing and upper-body work

A feel for the water

Imagine an Olympic track star psyching up for a long jump. He knows the crowd is watching, but his brain and nerve cells must shunt that film and soundtrack aside, along with all other distractions. Those receptors must block the constant bombardment of external stimuli—the color of the sky, perhaps a smell of smoke in the air, the feel of the track underfoot—and his internal regulatory functions go on automatic pilot so that everything focuses on the task at hand. His body will continue to fight gravity, whether he stops to marvel at it or not, just as he will keep breathing without being consciously aware of doing so.

Finally, the long jumper can literally no longer hear the crowd, and his vision tunnels in toward the pit straight ahead. He sprints and leaps—and the second he lands, his senses immediately reopen to register the roar of the crowd and his own heartbeat.

Dr. John C. Lilly experimented with this sensory-deprivation state during the 1950s by immersing his subjects in water to see what happened when the body had various assaults on its senses sharply curtailed and its perpetual battle against gravity relieved. He uncovered an astounding paradox. Instead of the "blank dull

TONY CARANNANTE AND RACE CONSULTANTS, INC.

A fishbowl full of starters at the second annual Major Walter Murphy
Memorial Triathlon in Staten Island, New York, in August 1983.

brain" effect one might expect, immersion produced a waking
dream state, as with the long jumper, in which solutions to
problems and remarkable achievements could appear out of
nowhere, suggesting that creativity could spring from a tabula-
rasa condition perhaps even more readily than through a kaleido-
scopic flood of imposed images.

If the $25-an-hour-and-up floating sessions in the sensory-
deprivation tanks that evolved from these studies seem a trifle
expensive, consider swimming in a cheaper isolation vat—open
water.

I mention all this because most would-be triathletes I've met
cite fear of vast water as their biggest stumbling block. In open
water you're literally over your head, with nothing to hold onto. If
you feel uneasy about running or cycling, after all, you can simply
stop.

In order to become rhapsodic about open water, you must first
unlearn the fears you certainly didn't have at birth. Dr. Igor
Charkovsky, an obstetrician at the Moscow Institute of Physical

Culture, conducted experiments in which he plunged infants only hours old into deep tanks of water. They played above and below the water's surface without panic, and were said to develop with more physical and emotional stability than other children. But try to throw a nonswimming adult new to cross-training—bristling with childhood warnings about undertow, sinkholes, and water snakes—into deep water!

Give yourself time to unravel any lingering aquaphobia you may suffer. Even if you're already a fair swimmer, sharpen your kinesthetic sensibilities when moving through water. Swimming should feel as natural as walking. Richard Marks, who swam the 26-mile Catalina Channel only 18 months after deciding to change his sedentary ways, offers succinct encouragement by saying, "Nonswimmers should realize that our bodies are about 65 percent water anyway. We're pretty much nothing but skin water balloons. Swimming is nothing more than a return to what we basically are."

If you are a cross-trainer with a swimming background

• At the risk of sounding like your aerobic astrologer, I want to say that you have tremendous self-discipline and incentive from putting in endless laps (whether or not you work out with a team, swimming is by its very nature solitary business). You know how to teach yourself to train and probably won't be the sort to bag a long run because your friend drops out after only 4 miles.

• Because your stroke is more efficient than the nonswimmer's, you'll enter the next segment of a triathlon with conserved energy and a head start.

• If you have a history of training in cool water, your body has developed high-grade thermoregulation. Acclimation to cold in-ures the body against constriction of blood flow to the extremi-ties, which fends off the cramping many runners and cyclists feel after a cold swim.

• Your strong abdominal muscles, spinal extensor muscles, and keen flexibility will ease the hunched-over position you must assume while cycling.

On the other hand

• Swimmers tend to have a higher percentage of body fat, which can impair running and cycling. As those other sports improve your body's ability to dissipate heat rapidly, however, the ensuing loss of extra body fat will cut down on your insulation in cold water.

• The muscle mass in your upper body may decrease as you spend more time with lower-body sports. Remember that this might mean slower pool times.

• You are accustomed to pushing hard but not to the impact trauma caused by running. Defer to the newfound soreness in your quadriceps and hamstrings.

• Since water continuously cools the body during swimming, you can sweat hard and never know it. The overheating in running and cycling will take some getting used to. "The basic difference between swimming and running," says Bill Phillips, an exercise physiologist at San Diego State University, "is body position. In running, the body is in a vertical position, and there is more hydrostatic pressure—the heart has to work harder to move the blood back to the heart for the circulation to be completed. In swimming, the body is horizontal, and so for people who are recovering from coronaries or who are beginning an exercise program, swimming is easier on them."

"Swimmers burn out early because they are used to incredibly hard, competitive work. Nonswimmers in a triathlon don't need to feel that pressure," says Brazilian Djan Madruga, a former Olympic swimmer who was ranked as one of the world's top 10 swimmers in 1982. "There's a tremendous mental boost in knowing that all you have to do is finish. You can come out of the water 15 minutes behind—about what it takes for champions to swim an entire mile—and make up for it quickly. You aren't thinking 'win.'"

Equipment

The basics

Suits: The Finals, a swimwear manufacturer, recently released a "Miraculon" suit. Because it's water-repellent and nonporous, it cannot be worn for more than 400 yards at a time, making it strictly a racing accoutrement—but also evidence of the growing specialization in swim accessories.

Begin with durable basics, and shop in specialty or sporting-

A swimmer in a tri-suit heads into the transition area to begin the cycling portion of the United States Triathlon Series race in San Diego, 1983.

good stores that offer racing suits. Steer clear of department stores. A skin-fitting Lycra model is fine for training and competition. A nylon suit is minimally heavier, slightly cheaper, and longer lasting.

Goggles: Finding the best style is largely by trial and error, since it's impossible to conform one shape to every individual facial bone structure. Some models come with padding around the lenses to ease the usual rift between you and the elements, but don't expect a flawless, leakproof seal all the time. (Some stores will let you try them on to ensure proper fit.) Lenses may be ordered to fit a corrective prescription; they come in a wide array of colors—from clear or amber to purple or red.

The best and cheapest way of preventing foggy lenses, incidentally, is wiping them with spit, antifogger of champions, before swimming. Never try a new commercial antifogger before a race. All too often triathletes watch months of training go belly up because unfamiliar chemicals they figured might give them an edge on race day have given them a bad case of shut-eye.

Cap: Thin latex caps of any color are acceptable for routine training, but don "international orange" in open water. Some race directors opt for bright red or yellow. Wear two caps for added prevention of heat loss through the head in cold water. There is even a combined cap-and-goggles set that can be worn to rather frightening effect.

Recommended tools of the trade

Fins: Fins aren't allowed in competition, so don't become dependent on them. But they're an aid in increasing ankle flexibility and leg strength, especially if you're warming up to running or cycling.

Pull floats: Styrofoam buoys with adjustable tethers provide flotation for your legs and lower body, allowing you to isolate your arm and shoulder muscles for intense technique drills.

Kickboards: Try leg-strengthening exercises by holding onto a lightweight foam kickboard for timed intervals.

Hand paddles: In addition to adding water resistance during your pull and recovery, drills with hand paddles encourage complete arm extension and stroke follow-through.

Drag suits: James E. Counsilman designed a suit with porous pockets that fits around the waist to catch water and slow you down. The faster you try to swim, the harder the drag makes you work. Competitive swimmers vary this theme by wearing two regular suits at once. Then, on race day, the sleekness of one suit adds the same psychological push as shaving.

A few eccentric gadgets

Swimming Walkman: Pace yourself with Handel's water music. Scott Molina swears by portable cassette players, but many coaches and athletes find them bothersome.

Swimmer's treadmill: An enclosed, tethered system that allows you to simulate free swimming by using a restraining belt and elastic cords is perfect for rich triathletes in cold climates. Add a wind-load simulator (indoor cycling apparatus) and runner's treadmill and become healthy as all outdoors without ever leaving your living room.

Stretching

Stretching expert Bob Anderson presents some preliminaries.

Swimming Stretches

1. In a standing or sitting position, interlace your fingers above your head. Now, with your palms facing upward, push your arms slightly back and up. Feel the stretch in arms, shoulders, and upper back. Hold stretch for 15 seconds. Do not hold your breath. This stretch is good to do anywhere, anytime. Excellent for slumping shoulders.

2. With arms overhead, hold the elbow of one arm with the hand of the other arm. Keeping knees slightly bent (1 inch), gently pull your elbow behind your head as you bend from your hips to the side. Hold an easy stretch for 10 seconds. Do both sides. Keeping your knees slightly bent will give you better balance.

3. The next stretch is done with your fingers interlaced behind your back. Slowly turn your elbows inward while straightening your arms. An excellent stretch for shoulders and arms, this is good to do when you find yourself slumping forward from your shoulders. This stretch can be done at any time. Hold for 5–15 seconds. Do twice.

4. Hold a towel near both ends so that you can move it with straight arms up, over your head, and down behind your back. Do not strain or force it. Your hands should be far enough apart to allow for relatively free movement up, over, and down. To isolate and add further stretch to the muscles of a particular area, hold the stretch at any place during this movement for 10–20 seconds.

5. A stretch for the arms, shoulders, and back. Hold onto something that is about shoulder height. With your hands shoulder width apart on this support, relax, keeping your arms straight and your chest moving downward, and your feet remaining directly under your hips. Keep your knees slightly bent (one inch). Hold this stretch 30 seconds. This is a good stretch to do anywhere, at anytime.

6. Sit on your feet, with your toes pointed behind you. Do not let your feet flare to the outside. If your ankles are tight put your hands on the outside of your legs on the floor and use your hands for support to help you maintain an easy stretch. Do not strain. Hold for 15–30 seconds. Be careful if you have or have had a knee problem.

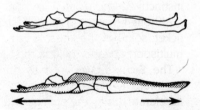

7. Relax with your knees bent and the soles of your feet together. This comfortable position will stretch your groin. Hold this for 60 seconds.

8. Straighten out your arms and legs. Point your fingers and toes as you stretch as far as you can. Stretch and then relax. This is a good stretch for the entire body. Hold for 5 seconds. Do three times.

To complement the swimming stretches, use 4–6 stretches for the back, hips, and legs from the cycling and running routines.

CREDIT: BOB ANDERSON
ILLUSTRATIONS BY JEAN ANDERSON

Techniques and innovations

Not long ago, swimmers lifted their heads straight up in order to breathe. "But I figured our mouths weren't on the top of our heads," said Jam Handy several years ago when he was 92. Handy's crusade to streamline the crawl took him to the Chicago Athletic Club in 1905 for 3 A.M. sessions dedicated to smoothing the awkward up-and-down movements of swimmers.

He played a substantial role in popularizing the turned-head pattern we now take for granted, and he pioneered the use of video equipment to dissect technique. Handy went on to develop picture simulators (called Jam Handys) to train World War II pilots on the ground. Driver's-education simulators are a direct offshoot of his audiovisual explorations. Swimming, meanwhile, underwent constant modifications and embellishments as a result of videotaping.

Films of Mark Spitz swimming are a case in point. Spitz had no idea that he wasn't pulling his arms through the water the "right" way, but coaches who watched him planing through the water discovered that he had such an inherent feel for the water that his stroke was revolutionary. They could then name what he knew instinctively and teach it to other swimmers.

Although the bottom line is that whatever works for you is the ticket, some of the latest keys to the stroke efficiency crucial to multisport athletes include the following.

The S-curve: We used to think that pushing water directly backward to set off a column of turbulence helped the arm accelerate during the pull, but videotapes of champion swimmers showed otherwise. Instead of circling their arms around like a windmill, they pulled their hands inward along an imaginary line down the center of their bodies, following an elliptical path. They carved an "S-curve" by seeking out still water, instead of water already moving, for greater propulsion.

Blading: Instead of slapping your hands down straight through the water, your hand should knife in thumb first at about a 45-degree angle. You don't want to slow yourself down by pushing a cupped hand of air into the entry point.

Elbows up: Dropped elbows are one of the most common energy wasters in swimming. If your elbow travels backward

HARALD JOHNSON

Feel the Water. Keep the pressure of the water on the fingertips and *feel* the water with your hand. If you don't maintain the pressure of the water on your hand as you stroke, you are pulling inefficiently.

One of my favorite stroke drills is called "catch up" because it gives me an opportunity to focus on the complete pulling phase of the stroke and the feel of the water, one arm at a time. This is how it works:

Push off from the wall with both arms extended in front of you. Pull through with one arm, but do not begin pulling with the other until you have completed your over-water recovery and actually touched it—the extended arm—in front of you. Then repeat the same procedures with the other arm and continue, breathing normally as needed throughout the length of the pool. You'll find you need to kick more while doing this drill.

---

before your hands, you're not pulling efficiently. "As your palm enters the water," says Madruga, "your elbows should be shoulder high. Then at the end of your stroke think of splashing water back up to the sky to emphasize hand acceleration."

HARALD JOHNSON

Chin up: That black line at the bottom of the pool may feel as if it's goading you onward, but try looking forward toward the wall you're approaching for a more streamlined position. Don't tuck your chin into your chest. Besides, when you swim in open water

Break the freestyle stroke into five separate and distinct parts: place, press, pull, push, and recover. These pictures single out one particular aspect of each of these components for you to concentrate on in order to improve your overall technique.

1. **Place.** Think "little finger first" as you place your recovery hand and arm in the water and roll onto that shoulder. The hand should enter shallow and stay shallow, extending out until the elbow is almost locked. At the end of this extension, your hand should be only 2–4 inches below the surface of the water, allowing the optimum pulling distance per stroke.

2. **Press.** At the top of your stroke, when your arm is fully extended in front of you, flex your wrist, then your elbow, to begin pressing against the water. Lead with your hand throughout the rest of your stroke.

If "place" and "press" are executed properly you can gain up to 12 inches of "pull" per stroke.

3. **Pull.** Imagine that the water is solid, and that your hand is pushing against something still as it moves down the length of your body during your pull—almost as though you are pulling your body over your hand.

Jack Nelson, coach of the Fort Lauderdale Swim Team, has swimmers pull themselves the length of a long rope or cord underwater (as though they are swimming) to help them get a feel for this important swimming principle.

4. **Push.** Follow through your stroke completely. Begin to push when you can no longer pull. Accelerate the speed of your hand at the end of your stroke just before it comes out of the water for recovery.

5. **Recover.** High elbows. Use this phase of the stroke to relax the hand and forearm muscles that have been working during the underwater pull. Lift the elbow high out of the water and let the forearm and hand follow. High elbows during recovery are hard to achieve unless you have the proper body roll.

Using a one-arm freestyle drill forces you to roll onto the arm and shoulder that are outstretched in front of you. It gives you a good feel for body roll and high elbow recovery. It is simple to do—just push off and swim using one arm only, keeping the other extended in front of you.

CREDIT: PHOTOS BY HARALD JOHNSON: REPRINTED BY PERMISSION OF BRUCE FURNISS, 1984.

the kelp won't cooperate by lying out in neat guiding lines, and you'll need a more "heads-up" reflex to stay on course anyway.

Kicking: Kicking hard won't speed you along but will definitely drain off more energy than it's paying out in dividends. Swim with

Head Position. As you swim, your head should be at about a 30-degree angle to the water—so that the water hits at the middle of your forehead just above your eyebrows. This head position allows your shoulders to ride slightly higher in the water, which creates much less resistance to the water and eases body roll and breathing. As your body rolls during your stroke, your head rolls with it to breathe. Do not lift your head or chin to breathe—just roll.

Building. Think of every lap you swim as having a short life of its own—a beginning, middle, and end. In the beginning, get your stroke together by concentrating on efficiency. Then, while maintaining that efficiency, start building—like kettledrums building to a crescendo—by increasing your kick and turnover rate so that you actually increase your speed as you swim the length of the pool.

This concept is part of a much larger picture. You should "build" every length, every series, every set, every workout.

Every stroke also has this same beginning, middle, and end. The hand speed of the freestyle pull should accelerate underwater building to an explosive push at the end of the pull.

Kicking. Boil the water, don't splash it. Kicking drills done without a board force you to kick underwater and increase your kicking efficiency. Put your arms out in front of you and use your hands as a board—try to "plane" on them as though they were a board. Feel free to use fins if you want to. At first you will probably find it necessary to bend your elbows slightly in order to stay afloat. As you progress, strive to lock them straight in front of you. Keep your thumbs locked—no sculling allowed.

HARALD JOHNSON

your upper body and relegate kicking to helping you stay balanced. Rev up your kicking drills, however, to strengthen your legs or to redirect blood in preparation for an upcoming segment of cycling or running (see Transition 1).

Bruce Furniss, former world record-holder in the 200-meter freestyle and 200-meter individual medley, and winner of two gold medals at the 1976 Montreal Olympics, believes that triathletes should try to master every trick it takes in learning how to take fewer strokes per lap in order to get more (for less energy) out of their swims. "Many triathletes lose interest in their swimming workouts or fail to improve because they just swim—repeating the same laps, the same workouts, the same way, day after day. They may swim hard, but they're just spinning. Avoid that pitfall by picking out something in particular to work on at every workout. Then you'll find that swimming is a constant challenge and that you always improve."

The aerobic base

Even though you are interested in long-distance swimming, not sprinting, many triathletes recommend reserving the lion's share of LSD work for cycling. "Once you can swim your goal distance," says Madruga, "don't waste time lap swimming. Switch to quality work."

"I do all interval work in the pool," says Mark Wendley. "That way I can reserve most of my over-distance cross-training for sports that pose a greater risk of injury when doing intervals."

To understand how *time versus distance* can work even when you're doing over-distance swimming while building up your aerobic stress base, consider the psychological effects of taking an untimed mile and turning it into a broken swim. Instead of loping back and forth for 66 lengths (a swimmer's mile), break it into 11-10-9-8-7-6-5-4-3-2-1 lengths. You'll have a great surge of incentive as you tire toward the end of your swim, because the decreasing numbers end up as a powerful spur.

Bob Krotee, an experienced triathlete and formerly an assistant swim coach at the University of Maryland, offers triathletes a number of swimming gears to maximize pool time.

___

Swim Tricks

Pyramids

Pyramids are a method of training in which you swim one length of the pool, build up to a specified number of lengths, and then decrease to one length. Rest 5–10 seconds between each segment. If you're tough, climb out and do five push-ups or five sit-ups between each segment.

When doing a 1-2-3-4-5-6-5-4-3-2-1 pyramid, you may be tired when you hit 6, but as the numbers decrease it seems to give you a psychological edge to push harder. It's simply a more efficient way of counting laps. Also, the rest time between each segment allows the body to practice working closer to its anaerobic threshold, meaning the length of time it can function without renewed oxygen intake. The higher your aerobic conditioning, the greater your anaerobic threshold. For example:

$\triangle$ 6 (1-2-3-4-5-6-5-4-3-2-1) = 36 lengths = 900 yards
Swim 25 yards and then rest 5–10 seconds, followed by 50 (rest), 75 (rest), 100 (rest), 125 (rest), 150 (rest), 125 (rest), 100 (rest), 75 (rest), 50 (rest), and finally 25 (rest) for a total of 36 lengths, or 900 yards.

$\triangle$ 8 (1-2-3-4-5-6-7-8-7-6-5-4-3-2-1) = 64 lengths = 1600 yards
Since eight lengths is 200 yards, work up to it in 25-yard increments as follows:

Swim 25 yards and then rest 5–10 seconds, 50 yards (rest), 75 (rest), 100 (rest), 125 (rest), 150 (rest), 175 (rest), 200 (rest); then progress back down by 25-yard increments. (You'll have more of an incentive to push yourself as the numbers decrease.)

Ladders

Ladders are similar to pyramids, except that each "rung" of the ladder equals 100 yards (or 50, 150, 200, etc.). Rest 15–30 seconds between each rung. For example:

100-200-300-400-300-200-100 = 64 lengths = 1600 yards
Swim 4 lengths and then rest 15–30 seconds, followed by 8 lengths (rest), 12 lengths (rest), 16 lengths (rest), 12 lengths again (rest), 8 (rest), and finally 4 (rest).

Broken Swims

For broken swims, take a specified distance and divide it into a variety of segments. For example:

Broken 1650 yards = 11-10-9-8-7-6-5-4-3-2-1 lengths
Instead of monotonously counting 66 laps, swim 11 (275 yards), 10 (250 yards), 9 (225 yards), etc., down to one length (25 yards). Rest 5–10 seconds between segments. You'll be working at a greater capacity as you near the end of the set than you would if you were simply swimming long distance.

Broken 2000 yards = 4 × 20 lengths
(rest interval: 45 seconds between segments) Swim 20 lengths four times for a total of 2000 yards. Rest 45 seconds between each segment.

Interval Training

Try swimming a prescribed distance a specified number of times on a constant time interval. For example, to swim 20 × 50 @ 1 minute, (as below), swim 50 yards 20 times, leaving every minute. If it takes you 51 seconds for the first 50, rest 9 seconds then begin the second 50 in the set. Repeat for all 20.

Repetitions		Distances		Interval
20	×	50 yards	@	1 minute
10	×	100 yards	@	2 minutes
6	×	200 yards	@	3:30

These are hypothetical examples. You will need to make your interval times longer or shorter, depending on your level of ability. The key is to allow yourself 5–15 seconds, rest—or whatever works best for you.

Fartlek Training

Change pace every so often to increase intensity. For example:
Swim 1000 yards; surge every fourth length.

Negative Splitting
   Do the second half of a given swim faster than the first. For example:

Swim 1600 yards:
   First 800 yards: 11:00 completion time; second 800 yards: 10:30 completion time.

Swim 4 × 50:
   First 25 yards: 0:32.00 completion time; second 25 yards: 0:30.00 completion time.
   Repeat three times to complete the set.

Get-Out Swims
   If you can do an outstanding time for a certain distance, give yourself the rest of the practice off. This is a good way to monitor your progress and a great way to avoid feeling guilty for not doing the yardage that you should.

CREDIT: BOB KROTEE

Other gears

Long-interval sets (100, 200, and 500 yards instead of fast sprint sets emphasizing 25s, 50s, and 100s) will teach you invaluable lessons in pacing. The shorter your rest time, the greater the effects on endurance. The longer the rest, the higher the quality of the swim because the heart rate is allowed more recovery time. When a swimmer in my lane once remarked, "Those fast guys aren't so hot. Look how long they rest!" he didn't realize that they were definitely in more pain than we were. Not only were they sprinting much harder for longer distances—they also had to be in top condition to push back up to sprint speed after allowing that recovery time.

"If you swim a set of ten 100s with short rest, aim to make the last 100 as fast as the first," advises triathlete Jennifer Hinshaw. "Spend most of your swimming time in the pool pacing yourself with the clock. Then you can transfer that sense of timing to open water."

Pacing

"Everyone should be aware how each individual stroke should feel in order to produce a given speed," says Chris Georges, coach of the Westside Masters Swim Team in Culver City, California, and editor of Swimming Technique magazine. "But how do you know what kind of pace you're holding out there in the middle of

HARALD JOHNSON

In timing your swim to determine your optimal aerobic training pace, you will need a pace clock and a friend with a lap counter to keep track of the distance you have covered. Immediately after ceasing exercise, count your pulse for 10 seconds and compare with your target rate. By comparing your pulse rate with elapsed exercise time and target rate, you can judge the intensity of your workout. Two minutes later another check of your pulse should show considerable recovery —a 10-second count of less than 20 is desirable.

the Pacific when there's no pace clock—nothing but blue water and blue sky?"

Georges suggests discovering your approximate swimming pace by using the formula introduced by Norwegian physiologist and coach Ørjan Madsen:

1. Swim 15–20 minutes (or 35–40, if you're tough) at top speed.
2. Record your time, and then divide it by the number of 100-meter (or -yard) segments you swam.
3. This number is your basic aerobic training pace.
4. Since one of your goals is to increase this pace, retest yourself every two weeks.

"Discover your pace by watching the clock during practice and then immediately making the connection between the time on the clock and the way the just-completed swim felt," says Georges. When you're ready to swim in open water, the only clock available will be this inner sensory-deprivation sense you've developed.

Special open-water considerations

Most triathlons are held in a lake or ocean because the crush of several hundred people awaiting staggered starts in a six-lane pool would quickly disintegrate into a melee resembling the scene at Times Square on New Year's Eve. Some skilled athletes don't bother with open-water training. "Swimming is swimming," shrugs Bill Ruth. For most of us, though, it's tough enough on race day without the added angst stirred up at the sight of pounding surf.

If like most people you do not live with easy access to safe open-water swimming, get to a race site as early as you can—several days to two weeks—to test the waters. Even lake swimming in preparation for an ocean contest will help. In the meanwhile, several skills can be practiced in a pool first.

Alternate breathing

You'll need to check course markings and assorted landmarks off to your right and left during an open-water swim, and that requires bilateral breathing. "At first it's like trying to write with your left hand if you're right-handed," says Michael Garibaldi, a former coach at the University of Utah who holds most of the records for swimming in San Francisco Bay. "Try breathing every third stroke—breathe to the right, take a stroke, breathe to the left—and remember that it's like driving a stick shift or doing flip turns. You have to get a thousand tries under your belt before you catch on."

Drafting

Drafting is strictly forbidden during cycling, but knowing how to draft during swimming can reduce your energy output by as much as 10 percent. "It's been an ocean-swimming secret for the last few years," says Harald Johnson. "The swimmer in the back gets the advantage, but the one in front isn't hurt. Position yourself directly behind a faster swimmer, and let yourself be pulled along in that person's slipstream. Watch for friends who swim by, and pace each other along by trading places."

The water-polo stroke

Don't waste energy by straying off course. Spot the buoys, trees, or landmarks beforehand that will give you your bearings. Then, every 5–10 strokes, lift your head by arching your back, emphasizing your kick so you won't lose speed, and check your position. If you don't see your landmarks, forget it that go-round. Don't paddle along frantically trying to glance at them every time. Put your head back in and try again at the next lift.

"This 'water-polo stroke' is tiring," says champion open-water enthusiast Marianne Brems, author of several swimming manuals. "But it'll become easier with practice. It's better than wasting time swimming in the wrong direction and then becoming reoriented by treading water or breaststroking. Don't count on other swimmers to steer you straight, either. They could be leading you anywhere."

Try swimming a few laps in the pool with your eyes closed. If you keep hitting the lane ropes, your stroke might be crooked enough to make you veer off sharply once you're let loose in the wilds. Work on straight, bilaterally strong stroking to save yourself the debilitation of needless armstrokes.

First ventures into open water

Consider going from the pool to open-water swimming the same as making the leap from city driving to freeway or open-highway cruising. Replace the stops and starts of interval training in the pool with the "open-road" feeling in boundless stretches of free water. That's the lure and beauty of the sport, but it requires more diligent safety guidelines.

1. Never, under any circumstances, swim alone. This rule has been drummed into our skulls since childhood, but it will always hold true no matter how expert you become. Don't assume that when you become competent it can be waived. Novices should find a swimming partner more skilled than they.

2. Counsilman enjoys a mammoth breakfast before a long swim, thereby laying yet another wives' tale to rest. Don't experiment with this the first time you're in open water. Many swimmers initially experience discomfort when they get into the water after eating, but after a number of tries they learn to use the food for energy. Find out what works for you; assume for now that you must wait at least half an hour after eating.

3. Don't swim at night. Sunlight helps you orient your position in the water. Similarly, don't swim in troubled water or in a rainstorm, because water conducts electricity.

4. Always come in from the cold. Hypothermia can sneak up on you as an insidious sensation of relaxation. You won't actually *feel* cold. If numbness, exhaustion, dizziness, or a passive and relaxed feeling descends, get out immediately. Most drownings occur within 15 meters of safety because the swimmer loses all notions of time and direction.

5. Never swim in abandoned quarries or secluded creeks or streams, and don't get romantic about an unguarded swimming hole. Confine your open-water swimming to lakes, ponds, rivers, bays, and parts of the ocean that have a safe bottom with gentle, gradual descents from the shallow to deep areas. The bottoms should be free of silt, logs, boulders, glass, metal, and sinkholes. Find shores that are free of litter and are well-raked.

6. Find areas with buoys, booms, or lifelines marking the areas safe for swimming. Reserve your training for areas supervised by trained personnel, but keep your experienced swimming friend along with you at all times anyway.

7. Wear a bright red or orange swimming cap so you can be spotted from shore, and try two caps to reduce the water's chilling effects.

8. Apply petroleum jelly to your armpits and thighs to prevent chafing, and the bewhiskered among you should also slop some on your shoulders to guard against sandpapering off a patch of skin from turning your head to breathe.

9. "If you ever have any hesitation about getting in, don't," says Garibaldi. "It's bigger than you and a lot stronger. Develop a healthy respect rather than a fear of it. Don't take a macho attitude to overcome your fears—you'll only end up intimidated. Macho guys are the first to get in trouble. I've backed off at times when I felt the surf was too high or the water was too cold." This is a man who has repeatedly swum from Alcatraz Island to San Francisco, a waterway thought to be impenetrable by those who designed the famous penitentiary, so you are in expert company should you want to back off without losing face.

Garibaldi offers novice triathletes hands-on guidelines to dealing with this unfamiliar training.

1. If you're going to swim in an ocean during a race, try a lake first. They're generally calmer and will accustom you to the idea of trying the ocean.

2. Enlist the aid of an experienced open-water swimmer who's about your pool speed. Ask around and read "places-to-go" listings in swimming magazines. Find out where the safest places to swim are in your vicinity (try to find roped-off areas), and approach the water together.

3. Salt water makes you more buoyant than fresh, but it won't make you ride the crest of the waves. Wait for less surf.

4. The water may feel considerably colder than you imagined. You may find yourself automatically hyperventilating. If that happens, consciously tell yourself to relax and get control of your breathing. Take several sessions in which you just teach yourself to adjust to cold-water sensations, without even attempting a bout of swimming.

5. Don't try to tackle too much. One-quarter mile is plenty at first. You need to get used to the taste of salt, and although your fears of sharks and jellyfish may be unfounded, you must have enough calm immersion time to work those suspicions out of your mind.

6. Wear fins for practice. They'll instill greater confidence and speed, as if you have the added boost of an outboard motor. Be prepared to doff them before a competition.

7. Don't swim out from shore. Beginners shouldn't attempt to make it "out to that buoy and back." Instead, swim parallel to the shore, so that if you feel uneasy at any time, you're close enough simply to head for terra firma.

8. To do that, *get beyond the surfline*. "It's like that first lane of traffic on the freeway," says Garibaldi. "Merging in and out of that is tougher for beginners than immediately jumping over into a cruising lane. The hard part is going through the surfline. Practice getting in and out, and restrict yourself to parallel-shore swimming beyond the choppy waves."

9. To swim in a straight line, get help from the ripples in the sand when the water is clear. They almost always run parallel to shore.

10. The waves and choppiness can defeat attempts at establishing a smooth rhythm. Keep your arm recovery higher than it would be in a pool.

11. Develop a support group even for your training swims. Knowing that a watchful eye is waiting there with a towel or blanket can add a sense of security.

12. Think of open-water swimming as new and exciting! You're doing this because you want to, not because you have to. Have a sense of conquering something you've never done before. Have your buddy-system compatriot teach you about how to watch for currents, undertow and all other raptures of the deep, and then realize that time and supervised help will cure any hesitation. There are also an increasing number of triathlons featuring pool swims or short lake swims, often sponsored by city recreational departments.

Manuals

Techniques, sample workouts, and background information.

James E. Counsilman
   The Complete Book of Swimming
   Atheneum, New York, 1977
James E. Counsilman
   The Science of Swimming
   Prentice-Hall, Englewood Cliffs, NJ, 1968
James E. Counsilman
   Competitive Swimming Manual
   Counsilman Co., IN, 1977
   Highly recommended
James Wagenvoord
   The Swim Book
   Bantam, New York, 1980
Marianne Brems
   Swim for Fitness
   Chronicle Books, San Francisco, 1979
Harvey S. Wiener
   Total Swimming
   Simon & Schuster, New York, 1980

Jan Prins
The Illustrated Swimmer
Honolulu He'e, Honolulu, 1982
Excellent for beginners
John Troup and Randy Reese
A Scientific Approach to the Sport of Swimming
Scientific Sports, Gainesville, FL, 1983
Ernest W. Maglischo
Swimming Faster
Mayfield, Palo Alto, CA, 1982

Periodicals

Swim Swim
P.O. Box 5901
Santa Monica, CA 90405
Prints "places to swim" directory
Swimming Technique
P.O. Box 45497
Los Angeles, CA 90045
Of interest to coaches and experienced swimmers
Swimming World and Junior Swimmer
P.O. Box 45497
Los Angeles, CA 90045
Age-group and senior swimmers

Organizations

Masters Swimming
A program for adult swimmers 25 and up (some clubs allow 19 and up). A good way to meet other swimmers and rapidly improve skills through organized workouts and informal meets. At present there is no central office. To find a chapter in your area, consult the "places to swim" listing in *Swim Swim* or call the various pools in your area—don't forget universities or junior colleges—to find out where they meet. Membership is $10.
National Young Women's Christian Association (YWCA)
600 Lexington Avenue
New York, NY 10022
(212) 753-4700
National Young Men's Christian Association (YMCA)
291 Broadway
New York, NY 10007
(212) 406-0090
Call the YMCA, YWCA, or Red Cross in your area for swimming lessons, special stroke clinics, or videotaping.

TRANSITION 1

I'll tell you how the Sun rose—
A Ribbon at a time—

—Emily Dickinson (1830–1886)

Swim-to-bike

The sunlight rising over the transition area in a triathlon illuminates a setting reminiscent of a surprise party waiting to happen. Colored flags, banners, and bicycles await the emergence of racers from the water. By the time the middle of the pack hits, the area looks like backstage at the school play. There's more to all this than wild clothes changing. Segueing from one sport to the next is a concept at the heart of cross-training.

"This isn't the time to be a quick-change artist," says Richard Marks. "Think instead of what the word *transition* means. You have to shift your focus, change direction, roll into another sport. This isn't the place to make up for lost time. It's when you should be getting your body ready to move into another exercise."

The physiological transition

Your circulatory system will shuttle blood to the muscles in use in order to bathe them in oxygen and clear away the lactic-acid buildup. That's why swimmers trying to climb up on a dock and onto a bicycle have sea legs so weak they wonder how they can stand up straight, much less punch out a few miles of cycling.

The cross-training trick is to redirect the blood pooled in the

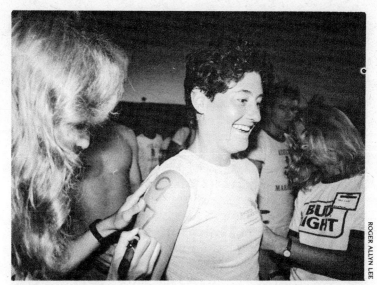

ROGER ALLYN LEE

Mary Jane Henning, No. 977, enjoys the ritual arm-marking before the 1982 Ironman as the sun begins to lighten the predawn sky.

upper body slowly toward the legs. Forcing the quadriceps and calves to work hard right away will only make them seem further beyond your command. Top triathletes switching from swimming to cycling will backstroke or breaststroke the final 100 yards or so toward the transition to get the blood pumping toward their legs.

Spectators at the 1983 Ironman were surprised to see Djan Madruga, the leader, seemingly coasting toward home port on his back. As swimming races go, he had yet another of his remarkable leads, but how could he have managed it if this was the way he lazed into the finish line? No final burst of energy toward the touchpad was happening here.

"I was doing a modified backstroke," says Madruga. "It imitates cycling in the water. Bring your knees all the way up toward your chest, emphasize your kick, and work your feet in a circular motion. That particular race I also tried a bit of freestyle with a breaststroke kick."

Other triathletes prefer to breaststroke their way in. Even so, you'll feel as if you're moving in slow motion at the beginning of your transitional cycling or running.

Transition keys

1. Kicking with fins or kickboard drills in the pool will strengthen your legs.

2. Swimming will shorten your lower back muscles, whereas flutter kicking will shorten the muscles in your calves. Stretch your legs and lower back after exiting the water.

3. Dave Scott warns that transitions in cold weather increase your susceptibility to injury because your muscles aren't as supple. For that reason, he recommends emphasizing individual activities to protect the muscular and skeletal systems instead of overloading yourself with back-to-back disciplines either when it's cold or when your muscles might be "cold" because you've fallen off from consistent training.

4. Swimming tightens your upper body. Stretch it to prevent tension during your cycling or running.

5. Remember that combination workouts change the effect of relative distances. A run after a swim needn't be as long as it would have to be on its own to arrive at the same aerobic conditioning.

Transition mechanics

"Don't bore yourself by actually practicing clothing change as a big part of your training," says Scott Tinley. "All it takes is having all your knickknacks laid out and ready to go."

1. Lay your cycling clothes out on your bicycle.

2. Keep a bucket of water near your bicycle, along with a towel, to rid yourself of dirt and sand that will wreak havoc on your feet if trapped in your cycling shoes.

3. Lace or pretie your shoes before swimming. New Velcro-closure cycling shoes are available.

4. Line your food up near your bicycle; try taping vitamin pills to the handlebars.

5. Watch the traffic on your way out of a transition area. The last thing you want to do is blaze out like a house afire only to crash into another cyclist.

6. Avail yourself of the showers in the area to prevent the irritation caused by salt water.

7. Don a helmet, wear gloves for protection, and don't forget sunglasses to cut down on glare.

8. Take time to apply sunscreen.

9. Start cycling with high revolutions per minute before shifting into racing gears.

10. Think of comfort instead of speed when making transitions.

11. Relax with transitions, and you'll give yourself a tremendous head start in shifting into the next sport.

Behold the life at ease; it drifts.
The sharpened life commands its course.
                                   —George Meredith (1828–1909)

Commercial diving was keeping me at sea around Singapore when I decided to take up cross-training. Twenty-five laps around the ship's steel deck equaled one mile. That's how I got dizzy from running, and I swam on the job. But I'd never competed or trained seriously before deciding to enter the October 1982 Ironman.

There I was in Hawaii on race day, after years on the high seas. So how come I got seasick during the swim? It was humiliating when they threw me a rope. I was like an infant, floundering all over, but I knew if I touched it I was out. I'd only been on a bicycle for 6 weeks before this, and it made me think, 'Oh, man, and swimming is my strong suit!' I finally struggled on deck in 601st place out of 850 racers, choking on salt water, sick as a dog.

Then something came over me. The bike was magic! Incredible! I jumped on it, mad at the ocean, and flew past 500 other athletes as if they were standing still. I went wild. I ended up with the 12th fastest cycling time that day, and 67th place overall in the race.

That did it. My father, an Episcopal minister, my mother, a journalist, and I discussed the situation. We decided to purchase a secondhand Winnebago motor home and go on the triathlon trail. One-man submarines used to be my specialty, but sometimes that mobile home felt like awfully close quarters. *Gamey* got to be my mother's favorite word.

But my parents were an unbelievable support team. We camped everywhere and met people all across the country. My father even took up cycling, using a bicycle I rebuilt for him practically from the wheels up. It's been an adventure we'll never forget.

                            —Bob Curtis, 25, formerly of
                              Hobart, Indiana
                              but now "getting maybe eight
                              miles to the gallon"
                              Commercial diver
                              Finished in a tie for 7th place at
                              1983 Ironman

CHAPTER 5

Cycling: Mental prowess and mechanical know-how

Don't bother to distinguish the outlandish story from the truth when it comes to cyclists. You'll hear legends about them eating chicken-fat sandwiches for fuel and about ultramarathons in which racers going on 2 hours of sleep their third day in a row burst into uncontrollable sobs for miles on end. They are as hell-bent as race-car drivers on swallowing the distance between two points faster than seems humanly possible, and if an outsider sees that as a touch eccentric—well, they're moving too fast to care.

This impulse has made cyclists the virtual standard bearers of an entire psychological sports phenomenon. *Breaking away* refers to the draw and ease of drafting that binds a pack of cyclists together like so much psychic glue. When anyone attempts to "break away" from the group, the others reel him or her in with their eyes and energies. It's like trying to pedal madly ahead while someone has hold of your suspenders. If you're on a straightaway, your feet will seem slow as molasses in response to the pack's inextricable hold. It takes rounding a corner or darting around some obstacle and out of the line of vision to slip free of this invisible tether.

The Oscar-winning movie *Breaking Away* was the story of a young cyclist trying to shake off these same restraining influences of his parents, school friends, and town. He needed that security of being held back, but he also needed to shake loose and find his own route. Cycling's actual "unseen reins" were the perfect metaphor to describe his growing pains, and he went back and forth riding with different groups and finally riding alone.

This balancing act between the benefits of group travel and the exhilaration of being a pacesetter marks the sport's core paradox: Bicycling lends itself more readily than swimming or running to an outing with friends or an organized tour, but the requirement of having to cover endless miles produces a mental acuity honed best in isolation. For potential cross-trainers, cycling is the surest way to harness the mental faculties required in any long endurance work.

Advantages and disadvantages

If you're already a competent cyclist

• Your sense of adventure enables you to deal with that sense of being many miles from home, giving you a handle on managing long distances, ultralong workouts, and emergencies while on the road.

• Cycling forces cross-trainers to learn energy conservation over long distances.

• Cycling helps maintain the elasticity of the blood vessels and benefits your legs, shoulders, back, diaphragm, and abdominals. It also improves digestion and overall muscle tone.

• Many triathlons have disproportionately large cycling segments to take full advantage of local scenery. Good cyclists often have the edge.

• Many doctors and exercise physiologists recommend cycling's leg-strengthening benefits for injured runners.

• You know how to soak up beautiful terrain in a skillfully paced and therefore less exhausted condition, giving your training an extra aesthetic air. Your senses are more alive to the world at large than when you swim, and more sweeping than when you run.

• You have that thrill of "speeding" known to downhill skiers or

Cyclists climb the course at Del Valle Regional Park near Livermore, California, during competition at the San Francisco regional race of the Bud Light U.S. Triathlon Series on July 10, 1983.

Olympic lugers, less so to swimmers or runners. A perfectly executed corner sweep is as breathtaking a daredevil move as you'll find in cross-training.

• You are your own mechanic. Being prepared to handle repair emergencies and keeping your machine ready for action instills confidence.

• Cycling will stretch out your lower back, strengthening it for swimming and running.

Cycling is Europe's most popular sport. Small wonder that Leonardo da Vinci was merrily sketching bicycles back in the fifteenth century. Now it's easier than ever in America to hit the road. Touring groups, special magazines, and bike paths have sprung up practically overnight.

On the flip side

• If you're one of those traditionally wiry cyclists, it may take a whirlwind of upper-body work to get into swimming shape, which may in turn reduce your cycling times.

• It's expensive. You don't have to plunk down $2000 if you're a novice, but $400–$500 is the lowest possible initiation fee for a serviceable bicycle. Cycling is furthermore an outfitting project— you'll need shoes, a helmet, and other colorful accoutrements. Of course, you can make it pay for itself if you forsake car-maintenance bills and parking fees by biking to work.

• Cycling is the most difficult cross-training sport to fit into a busy schedule. You can swim in a pool or run around a well-lit track after work, but a beginner who cycles on the road at night is tempting the gods. Get a wind-load simulator to use indoors.

• Being dependent on a machine has its disadvantages. Ask Mark Allen, who was hounding Dave Scott for the lead in the October 1982 Ironman when his rear derailleur snapped, ruining his year's training and a hard-charging run after the title. Even competent mechanics sometimes fall prey to malfunctions or flat tires that can put them out of the running.

• Unfortunately, what feels right to a beginner, such as pushing in high gear, is often a mistake.

• "Getting out the door is the hard part," says triathlete Marc Surprenant. Driving to the pool or strapping on running shoes and heading out the back door often feels easier than taking your bicycle off its moorings and weaving through an urban obstacle course.

• Cycling poses traumatic injury possibilities. As in gymnastics, beginners should learn how to fall. "It's an inevitable part of the sport," says triathlete Marc Thompson, a former Olympic cyclist. "Learn how to roll rather than trying to break a fall with your hands." Collarbone fractures are the most common serious cycling injury. Strength training will toughen the shoulder girdle muscles during your slow convalescence.

• Cycling clubs can sometimes be close-knit to the point of impenetrability, and beginners or triathletes aren't always welcome. Check with other triathletes for suitable cycling contacts.

Equipment

Put yourself right away into the hands of friendly, knowledgeable salespeople in a reputable shop. They are often cyclists themselves, unlike those who rove around large bicycle emporiums relegating an instrument's selling points to its color and shine. A smaller shop might not be cheaper in the short run, but they won't try to sell you a discount special that will be heavy to the point of uselessness. Establish rapport with someone who can help you with servicing later.

Other points to expedite your investment:

1. Decide how much you want to spend. Save those gleaming, expensive models for when you've ironed the kinks out of your cycling technique. Plan on spending $400–$500 (see "The Specs," pages 126–29, for suggested novice bicycles) for a stripped bicycle first.

2. Choose a light alloy frame (22–24 pounds with clincher tires, 21½–23 pounds with sew-ups).

3. You will want 10–12 gears, quick-release wheels, and components that are all alloys, from the pedal to the seat.

4. Pay attention to the water bottle fittings and other practical features, which are good indicators of the bicycle's quality. Steve Neely of Helen's Cycling Shop in Los Angeles also recommends a bicycle computer to give yourself an accurate reading of revolutions per minute (rpm), miles per hour (mph), miles covered, and pacing. A good model will cost about $50.

5. Decide whether you want a racing or touring bicycle. "The touring bike is more comfort-oriented," says Neely. "A racer is more sensitive to the road so that you know exactly when to apply the brakes. You can go fast knowing that you can sense anything amiss. A racing bike is like a sports car, a touring bike like a luxury car."

The racing bike is shorter and maximizes your pedal power. If you plan to consolidate or establish your position in the cycling leg of a triathlon, get a racing bike. Touring bicycles are longer, more flexible, and do a better job absorbing road shocks. Ask to see a touring model if you want to be a recreational rider instead of a competitor.

6. Look for a bike that's as light as possible.

The Specs: Training and Racing Models for under $525

Manufacturer, model, and manufacturer's suggested retail price	Frame construction and sizes available	Weight	Rims and tires	Brakes	Gearing	Accessories
Bianchi Limited $436–$439	Ishiwata double-butted chrome moly tubing. 19", 21", 22", 23", 24", 25"	22–22.5 pounds (21" frame)	Araya alloy rims, clincher tires.	Dia Compe 500G side-pull.	12-speed 42/52 crankset 14-28 cluster	Toe clips and straps; water bottle cage.
Bridgestone Triathlon A. L. $375–$400	Double-butted chrome moly tubing. 19", 21", 23", 25"	24 pounds (23" frame)	Araya alloy rims, clincher tires.	Bridgestone self-centering side-pull.	12-speed 42/52 crankset 14-28 cluster	Toe clips and straps; water bottle cage fittings.
Centurion Elite 12 $365	Tange double-butted chrome moly tubing. 19¾", 21", 23", 25"	23.75 pounds (21" frame)	Araya alloy rims, clincher tires.	Dia Compe New GT-400 side-pull.	12-speed 42/52 crankset 13-28 cluster	Toe clips and straps; water bottle cage.
Team Fuji $425	Quad-butted chrome moly tubing. Centimeters: 52, 55, 58, 61, 64	23 pounds (55 cm. frame, approx. 21½")	Ukai alloy rims, clincher tires.	Dia Compe 500G side-pull.	12-speed 42/53 crankset 13-26 cluster	Toe clips and straps; water bottle cage fittings.
Gitane Criterium $449	Vitus 971 double-butted tubing. 20½", 22½", 24½"	23.1 pounds (22½" frame)	Mavic alloy rims, clincher tires.	Weinmann 405 side-pull.	12-speed 42/52 crankset 14-24 cluster	Toe clips and straps; water bottle and cage.

Model	Tubing	Weight	Rims/Tires	Brakes	Gearing	Accessories
KHS Triathlete $499–$525	Reynolds 531 double-butted tubing. 21″, 23″, 25″	22.9 pounds (21″ frame)	Araya Aero ADX-IW rims, clincher tires.	Dia Compe New Gran Compe side-pull.	12-speed 42/52 crankset 13-24 cluster	Toe clips and straps; water bottle cage fittings.
KHS Turbo $349–$365	Tange double-butted chrome moly tubing. 19″, 21″, 22″, 23″, 25″	23.2 pounds (21″ frame)	Araya alloy rims, clincher tires.	Shimano 600EX side-pull.	12-speed 42/52 crankset 14-28 cluster	Toe clips and straps; water bottle cage fittings.
Kabuki Diamond Formula $400	Double-butted chrome moly tubing. 21″, 23″, 25″	21.5 pounds (21″ frame)	Araya alloy rims, clincher tires.	Bridgestone self-centering side-pull.	12-speed 42/52 crankset 13-24 cluster	Toe clips and straps; water bottle cage fittings.
Lotus Classique $392–$399	Tange double-butted chrome moly tubing. 19″, 21″, 23″, 25″, 27″	23 pounds (21″ frame)	Ukai alloy rims, clincher tires.	Shimano 600EX side-pull.	12-speed 42/52 crankset 14-32 cluster	Toe clips and straps; alloy water bottle cage.
Lotus Aero Sport $499–$509	Tange double-butted chrome moly tubing. Centimeters: 50, 52, 54, 56, 58, 60, 62, 64	23 pounds (52 cm. frame, approx. 20½″)	Araya Aero ADX-1 rims, clincher tires.	Shimano 600AX para-pull.	12-speed 42/52 crankset 14-28 cluster	Toe clips and straps; water bottle and cage.
Marukin Tri-Star $450	Ishiwata double-butted chrome moly tubing. 21″, 23″, 25″	20 pounds (23″ frame)	Ukai alloy rims, tubular tires.	Dia Compe 500G side-pull.	12-speed 42/52 crankset 14-24 cluster	Toe clips and straps; frame-fit pump.

Manufacturer, model, and manufacturer's suggested retail price	Frame construction and sizes available	Weight	Rims and tires	Brakes	Gearing	Accessories
Motebecane Jubilee Sport $320	Columbus double-butted chrome moly tubing. 21", 23", 25"	23.5 pounds (21" frame)	Mavic alloy rims, clincher tires.	Weinmann 506 side-pull.	12-speed 42/52 crankset 13-24 cluster	Toe clips and straps; water bottle cage fittings.
Nishiki Comp II $490–$495	Tange double-butted chrome moly tubing. 21", 23", 25"	24 pounds (23" frame)	Araya Aero ADX-1 rims, clincher tires.	Dia Compe Aero G side-pull.	12-speed 42/52 crankset 13-24 cluster	Toe clips and straps; water bottle cage fittings.
Panasonic Deluxe 2000 $320	Chrome moly tubing. 20", 22", 24", 26", 28"	25 pounds (22" frame)	Alloy rims, clincher tires.	Dia Coupe 500 side-pull.	12-speed 40/52 crankset 13-26 cluster	Toe clips and straps; water bottle and cage.
Peugeot PSV 10 $499	Reynolds 531 double-butted tubing. 21", 21¾", 22½", 23¾", 24", 25"	21 pounds (22" frame)	Mavic alloy rims, tubular tires.	Weinmann 605 side-pull.	12-speed 42/52 crankset 13-21 cluster	Toe clips and straps; water bottle cage fittings.
Puch SLE $459	Reynolds 531 chrome moly tubing. Centimeters: 53, 55, 57, 59, 63, 63.5	25.6 pounds (57 cm. frame, approx. 22½")	Weinmann 700 alloy rims, clincher tires.	Weinmann 506 side-pull.	12-speed 41/52 crankset 13-21 cluster	Toe clips and straps; water bottle and cage.

Model	Frame construction / Sizes	Weight	Rims / Tires	Brakes	Gearing	Accessories
Raleigh Competition $525	Ishiwata double-butted chrome moly tubing. 60, 63	25 pounds (60 cm frame, approx 23⅝")	Araya Aero ADX-1W, clincher tires.	Dia Compe Aero ACG300 side-pull.	12-speed 42/52 crankset 12-24 cluster	Toe clips and straps; water bottle cage fittings.
Ross Paragon $400	Tange double-butted chrome moly tubing. 19", 21", 23", 25"	23 pounds (21" frame)	Araya alloy rims, clincher tires.	Dia Compe 500G side-pull.	12-speed 42/52 crankset 13-21 cluster	Toe clips and straps; water bottle cage fittings.
Schwinn Super Sport $399	Double-butted chrome moly tubing. 19", 21", 23", 25"	23 pounds (21" frame)	Araya alloy rims, clincher tires.	Gran Compe 500G side-pull.	12-speed 42/52 crankset 13-26 cluster	Toe clips and straps; water bottle cage fittings.
SR Pro Am $458	Double-butted chrome moly tubing. 19", 21", 23", 25"	23 pounds (21" frame)	Araya alloy rims, clincher tires.	Dia-Compe New Gran Compe 400 side-pull.	12-speed 42/52 crankset 13-24 cluster	Toe clips and straps; water bottle cage fittings.
TREK 560 $419	Reynolds 501 double-butted tubing. 19", 21", 22½", 24", 25½"	23.25 pounds (22½" frame)	True America matrix rims, clincher tires.	Dia Compe Aero 500Q side-pull.	12-speed 42/52 crankset 13-24 cluster	Toe clips and straps; water bottle cage fittings.
Univega Gran Rally $390	Double-butted chrome moly tubing. Centimeters: 50, 54, 60, 63	23.5 pounds (50 cm. frame, approx. 19½")	Araya alloy rims, clincher tires.	Shimano 600EX side-pull.	12-speed 42/52 crankset 13-28 cluster	Toe clips and straps; water bottle cage fittings.
Univega Gran Premio $500	Double-butted chrome moly tubing. Centimeters: 50, 54, 57, 60, 63	23 pounds (50 cm. frame, approx. 19½")	Araya alloy rims, clincher tires.	Dia-Compe NGC-400 side-pull.	12-speed 42/52 crankset 13-26 cluster	Toe clips and straps; water bottle cage fittings.

Bicycles listed are based on 1983 prices and were not tested by publishers.
Information was supplied by manufacturers and their representatives in response to a questionnaire. Frame-construction column describes main tubes only. All wheel hubs are quick-release design, front and rear. To convert centimeters to inches, 1 inch equals 2.54 centimeters.

Now for a more detailed shopping spree. Here's an accessory starting kit for a novice:

Seats: Splurge on a good seat. All it will take is one blistering introduction to saddle sores from an improperly adjusted saddle to convince you that $50 is a small investment. You may feel like king of the hill sitting on a plastic throne cushioned by vinyl or some other padding there in the store, but rest assured it may end up being a real pain in the ass a few miles down the road.

Hard leather saddles in different sizes (wider models for women) require some patient breaking in, and are falling out of favor. They need to be oiled and cured in the sun before use, but it beats having your rear end do the groundbreaking ceremonies. Seats now come in adjustable sizes, and in many different grades of plastic, but any way you slice it, plan on being uncomfortable for a while. You wouldn't embark on a perilous hike in new boots, so take it easy in the saddle for a while.

Tires: You can buy sew-ups or clinchers. Sew-ups are casings with tubes sewn inside. Although hard to repair, they're the racer's choice because they're quickly pulled off and replaced with a new tire. They're also light enough that extras can be packed along. Be prepared to shell out $20–$40 at a crack.

Many bikes come with clinchers—casings with removable tubes. These cheaper, heavier tires will give beginners a more solid, "grounded" feeling. The more experienced you become, the more you'll want to look on the lighter side. Clinchers are easier to fix and only about $9–$12 each, but there's none of this fast-change business. Consider training with clinchers until your event, and then switch to sew-ups.

Small "tire savers" sell for about $1.25 each and attach to the brake bolts to fend off the insidious and unseen road hazards that your tires seem to attract like magnets.

Extras: Buy a tire pump, water bottle, toe clips, and a repair kit.

Gloves: "Wear gloves to protect your hands when you fall and on long rides to prevent nerve damage," says Marc Thompson. Every now and then as you ride, let go with one arm and shake it to keep the circulation going and relax your upper body.

Clothing: Since you've come this far, go all out and spring for some natty cycling shorts. You'll want all the comfort you can get, and for a $25–$50 price tag some are lined with chamois in the crotch and seat for comfort. They're cut long to prevent chafing and high in back for wind protection.

Cycling jerseys are specially designed for low wind resistance. Adjust your own ventilation with the jersey's zippered neck. During cold weather, new clothing configurations are necessary. Although less sleek costuming will slow you down, exposing yourself to the cold, particularly your knees, is an open invitation to muscle injury. Wear cycling tights or leggings.

When the weather is wet, replace those rain jackets that make you feel as if you're in a sauna with coverings made of Gore-Tex, a new, lightweight membrane laminated to fabric, resulting in all-weather garments.

Shoes: Cycling shoes are light but reinforced with a rigid sole to help you push the pedals. If the shoe fits, never mind socks. They're perforated for ventilation, but forget about going out for a leisurely stroll in them. Special cycling shoes for triathletes come with Velcro closures for quick transitions. "Buy cheap shoes to start," says Bob Curtis. "You can add Velcro yourself to save money." Ask your salesperson to recommend what shoe sole best suits your needs. As you become experienced, you'll want a cleated shoe for maximum power and efficiency.

Helmet: According to Fred Matheny, a top cyclist and author of *Beginning Bicycle Racing,* the 1982 Coors Classic cycling race, which featured some of the world's best riders, ended with so many head injuries that it fueled continuing debate over what constitutes a "safe" helmet.

"Many would-be racers associate plastic helmets with tourists—with slow, with incompetent. But style is just a matter of learned response," says Matheny. "If European pros had always worn hard shells, they would look right and other racers would follow suit. I suspect that soon the hard-shell helmets will become the norm, while the leather models will look as dated as Red Grange's football helmet."

"Spider helmets are a joke," agrees Bob Curtis. If you're already tired by swimming, you can't depend on your reflexes to be quick enough to avoid an accident.

Hard shells are designed to absorb impact, but the trade-off is that they offer far less ventilation than those leather-lattice jobs. Part of your energy is redirected into trying to cool off your scalp, but cyclists should be more concerned with keeping life and limb intact.

Fit to be tried

Now that you have a rough idea of what the animal looks like, you have to find one that fits. The average bicycle frame is 19–25 inches, which refers to the distance between the seat lug and the center of the bottom bracket. Don't think you can compensate for a frame that's too small by changing the height of the seat. You still won't be able to set the handlebars to a comfortable height.

According to Bill Bryant, owner of the Cupertino Bike Shop in northern California and a popular mechanic among triathletes, many bike shops carry "fit kits"—instructions listing tables and criteria for sizing yourself up. Although we all come in different shapes and sizes, here are some basic rules of thumb.

1. Measure your inseam—from the floor to your crotch—while you're standing barefoot.
2. Subtract 9–10 inches for your bicycle frame measurement.
3. Once in the store, straddle your "correct fit" model. With your feet on the floor (no shoes), the top tube of the frame should be about 1 inch from your crotch.
4. You may have to subtract an inch more to find your perfect match. A bicycle that's too big or too small will distribute your weight incorrectly.
5. A small person on a large frame will throw too much weight at the back end and not enough to the front, causing an unstable front wheel.

Steve Neely suggests another formula.

1. Take two-thirds of your inseam measurement to find your frame size.
2. If you have exceptionally large feet, increase the frame size by an inch. If your feet are small, decrease it a tad.

Then adjust the seat height.

1. Place the cranks at 12 and at 6 o'clock.

2. Keep your feet parallel to the ground.

3. When your saddle is correctly positioned, your knee should be slightly bent when you're seated, with one pedal in the 6 o'clock position. Too much of a bend will cause you to wobble from side to side as you pedal. If the seat is too high, you might as well go stick your knees into a threshing machine.

4. Keep the seat level or tilted forward a fraction of an inch. Tilting it downward will throw your body weight forward onto your handlebars.

5. The bicycle should accommodate your torso so that you don't have to strain to get to the handlebars, but it shouldn't be so compacted that you can't get into a racing position.

Tackle the height of your handlebars next.

1. Racers want to be as low as possible to have the least wind resistance, but if you're going for visibility in commuter traffic, you'll want slightly higher handlebars. "The handlebars should be 1½–2½ inches below the saddle," says Bill Bryant.

2. Adjust them by raising or lowering the stem without taking more than 2½ inches of stem out of the frame. Begin with the bars an inch below the saddle and take a short ride to assess how it feels.

3. Stems come in different extension sizes for riders with long arms, and handlebars come in flat or dropped design. You may find the dropped style uncomfortable at first, but once you adjust it will add tremendously to your training rides. The flat style is basically for the city pedaler.

4. Steel and alloy bars have different diameters, which might require you to change your bicycle stem if you want different handlebars. Have your shop ally make sure that you are buying new parts that will work together.

Pedal action

Any pedals will work as long as toe clips and straps can be attached. High-quality replacements run in the neighborhood of $15–$35, with alloy racing pedals selling for up to $100 a pair. Japanese models of the $60 Campagnolo road pedals cost about $25 a pair and are easy to find.

With high-quality pedals, the bearing surfaces are of high-temper metals adjusted for the least amount of friction between your shoe and the pedal. The bearings of inexpensive models will break down after the first few hundred miles of riding.

Toeing the line

"Toe clips allow novices—or anyone—to learn the full-circle pedaling that develops the cycling muscles you'll need," says Neely. "If you're only pushing the pedal in a downward motion, you're putting too much strain on your knees."

Although toe clips might fill you with premonitions of being trapped on a machine even as you streak headlong into peril, they are actually a helpful safety device. They'll keep your feet on the pedals at all times so that there's less chance you'll lose control of your bike.

Ride with the straps loosely adjusted at first until you lose your hesitation. "Try them out in an empty schoolyard or parking lot," says Scott Tinley. "You don't want to be fiddling with them while you're riding in traffic."

Wear your cycling shoes when you buy your bicycle to make sure the toe clips fit. They shouldn't rub against your shoe or chafe your toes. The toe strap weaves through the pedal, over the top of the foot, and then through a hole in the clip. The end of the strap goes into a buckle on the outside of your foot, where it can be reached for what should be minimal frantic tugging.

Derailleurs

The major manufacturers of derailleurs are Sun Tour and Shimano in Japan, and Simplex and Huret in Europe. Campagnolo offers state-of-the-art derailleurs for $150 and up; the Japanese and French companies make high-performance sets that operate well for less than half the price.

Cranksets

Your bicycle's cranksets should last a long time, although the bearings that hold the axle of the crankset inside the frame and the teeth of the chainwheels might wear out sooner. Inexpensive alloy cranksets will flex as you pedal; as you become more advanced, you'll find that wastes energy. You can change the chainwheels without replacing the entire mechanism if you have a high-quality crankset.

Most standard bicycles come with a 52-tooth chainwheel on the outside of the crankset, with 40 teeth inside for the lower gears.

Braking away

Brakes made of one of the softer alloys require more pressure to make them work, meaning that they wear out a good deal faster than more expensive models. Replace brake pads often, or supplement inexpensive brakes with expensive brake pads to prolong their usefulness.

All washed up:
Getting to know your machine

Once you've paid your money and taken your new bicycle home, the two of you are going to have to get along. "The best way to get the most out of your cycling is really to fall in love with your bicycle," says Kathleen McCartney. "It's not just a training tool, but a key to adventure. The more fun you have on your bike, the more you'll ride it; the more events you attend, the more good cyclists you'll meet."

The best possible way for cross-training cyclists to assume McCartney's tone of familiarity with a bicycle—a machine that can seem a mysteriously complex grab bag of otherwise unassuming parts—is through a ritual bathing. Washing rites are the most direct way to zero in on each area and component. You need immediate, hands-on contact to make it seem less a contraption and more an object of your affections.

Find a clean, well-lighted work area. You're more apt to discover malfunctioning or worn parts through this step-by-step care-taking, because only washing a bicycle allows you to make the close inspection necessary to detect frayed cables, loose parts, and fractures that might be hidden by excess dirt and grease. You'll also develop a positive attitude toward repairing as well as riding.

Bill Woodul, promotions manager for Specialized Bicycle Components, U.S. Olympic Team mechanic, and U.S. Cycling Federa-

tion Team mechanic for six world championships, provides novices with the following washing tour of their new machines (see
the photographs for details).

Frame: First, use a solvent and rag to remove excess grease
and built-up road dirt. Then go over the entire bicycle with soap

TRISHA O'RIELLY

and water, being careful not to spray water directly into the freewheel, bottom brackets, or hubs. Dry and polish it carefully and completely with a soft cloth, and lubricate the chain and brake mechanisms.

Wheels: Check the wheels first after cleaning the bicycle, because wheel repairs can be time-consuming and often require professional attention. Make sure the wheels are "true." A true wheel should spin freely with no lateral or vertical deviation.

Squeeze all spokes by hand, in pairs, to ascertain that none are

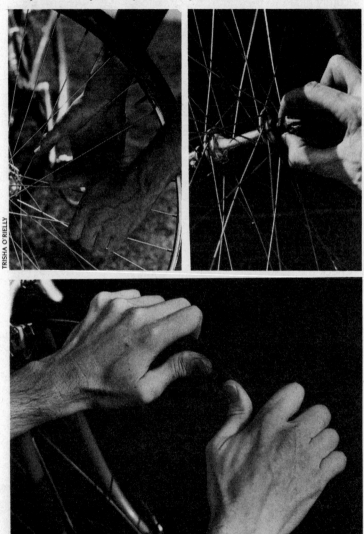

loose or broken. Remove the wheel and check the hub axle by rolling it with your fingers. There should be no play, and movement should be free and smooth. Examine each tire, including the spare, for tread wear, cuts, and bruises. Make sure the tire is securely glued to the rim by trying to force the tire to roll, using your thumbs.

Bars, stem, seat: With the bicycle in an upright position, straddle the rear wheel, facing forward. With sharp percussive movements, apply lateral and then up-and-down pressure to the seat to detect looseness.

Check the handlebars by straddling the front wheel, facing the rear of the bicycle, and applying percussive pressure to them. Check for movement of the bars within the stem as well as movement of the stem within the head tube. Then check the brake levers for secure attachment to the bars.

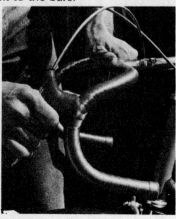

Derailleurs, cables, shift levers, chain: Place your bicycle on a rack or suspend it above the ground in some manner so that the rear wheel spins freely. With the wheel spinning, shift the gears from the extreme inner to the extreme outer position rapidly several times to ensure that all of the gears are operating.

Spin the wheel again and move the shift levers so that the chain rides on the inner (small) chainring in the front and the inner freewheel cog (largest diameter) in the rear. When the derailleurs are in this position, the lateral clearance between the inner cage plate of the front changer and the chain should be ⅛ inch for unobstructed operation.

Conversely, when the chain is on the outer freewheel cog and the outer chainring, there should be ⅛ inch clearance. There should also be ⅛ inch clearance between the bottom of the outer cage plate and the top of the teeth on the large chainwheel. There should be no slack in the gear-shifting cables.

After this "bench test," road test your bicycle. If the chain slips or skips under pressure, it might need lubrication. The chain might also be stretched out of shape or have a "stiff" link. The freewheel cog might be badly worn. In any case, replace the worn parts before serious riding.

Brakes, levers, cables: Squeeze the brake levers to test cable operation. Look for frayed, worn, or rusted cables, which should be replaced. The brake pads should fit properly to the rim and not be excessively worn. The pads should both touch the rim at the same time and have total contact with it. They should also "toe in" slightly (the front leading end of the brake touching the rim first). Correct any deviation from smooth, even operation.

Crankset, crankarms, bottom bracket: First, check the tightness of the crankarm fixing bolt, then slide the chain off the inside chainring and spin the unrestricted crankarms. The crank assembly should spin freely and quietly. Take a closer look at the bottom bracket bearing assembly if there's any noise or irregular movement. Check that the chainwheels are straight by spinning the cranks and watching for lateral deviation.

Next, check for excessive bottom bracket play by holding the pedal end of either crankarm (not the pedal) and trying to move it toward and away from the frame. Any lateral movement is excessive and requires adjustment of the bottom bracket.

Pedals, straps, toe clips: Check the pedals for smoothness of spin and for any lateral movement of the pedal on the pedal axle. Pedals should fit snugly against the crankarms.

Check the toe clips for cracks. The most common fatigue point is in the bend where the toe clips and pedals meet. Replace as necessary. Leather toe straps should be free of grooves and neither stretched nor worn thin; the buckles shouldn't be rusted.

Here's a quick once-over for a properly maintained bicycle

you're about to take out on the road from David Guettler, manager of the Bianchi-Vespa Bicycle Store in San Francisco.

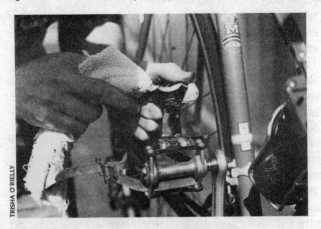

TRISHA O'RIELLY

1. Pick your bike up a few inches and drop it. It should drop quietly, without any rattling.

2. Spin the wheels. The brake shoes shouldn't rub on the rim, and the wheels shouldn't wobble.

3. Squeeze the brakes hard. You want to be absolutely certain that the brake cables aren't about to give way.

Flat out of luck:
If nothing else, learn this one maintenance job
Novice triathletes talk a lot about shaving seconds off their swimming times, but they never consider that knowing how to change a flat tire quickly can save them crucial minutes in a race. Sooner or later a blowout will strike, and chances are you're going to have to fix it yourself.

Deflect the inevitable for as long as possible by:

1. Keeping your tires inflated to the recommended pressure.
2. Replacing tires as soon as the treads begin to wear thin.
3. Steering clear of glass or metal in the road.
4. Brushing tires clean (while you're wearing gloves) whenever you stop.

When you get a flat despite all your good intentions, here's the best way to get down to business.

Sew-ups

1. Remove the wheel using the quick-release lever. Before you leave the bike store, find out how to operate this lever. While you're at it, learn how to operate the brake's quick release, which will enable you to loosen the brakes should they rub against the tire and prevent its smooth removal.

2. Locate the tire valve and release any trapped pressure.

3. Remove the tire, starting on the side of the wheel opposite the valve, slowly pulling it away from the metal rim. Apply glue to rim and allow to dry partially before you begin to stretch the new tire over it.

4. If you're on the road, get out your spare—a used tire with old glue on it. Insert the valve stem into the hole in the rim to which it belongs.

5. Press the rim against a clean surface, such as a patch of clean ground or a fence wall. Starting at the valve stem, stretch the tire onto the rim, using both hands. Gently stretch the tire around the wheel without using a metal object or pry bar.

6. Next, using the tire pump, inflate the tire to half-pressure. Check that the tire is on evenly. If it isn't, align it by twisting it around in either direction. Replace the wheel on the frame, lock the quick-release lever and reset the brake-release mechanisms. Then inflate the tire with your hand pump until it is hard when you pinch it with your thumb.

It sounds more complicated than it really is. With a few practice runs, the entire operation should take less than 5 minutes and only a trace of anxiety.

Patching a sew-up, however, is a more traumatic ordeal. Let your bicycle shop do it, or check a repair manual (Eugene A. Sloane's *Bicycle Maintenance Manual* is good for beginners) and settle in to do battle.

Clinchers

1. You'll need a pump, patch kit, and two tire irons. If you have quick-release axles, they'll be either on the handlebars or on the brake caliper of the wheel. Again, find out what you have and how it operates before you're out the shop door.

2. Use the quick-release lever to remove the wheel.

3. Pump some air into the tire so that you can spot the leak, and mark the area with a pen, pencil, or stone.

4. Use your hands or the tire irons to take the tire from the rim. Work one tire iron in between the rim and the side of the casing. Be careful not to cause a second leak by scraping the tire with the iron. With the first iron holding the tire in place, work the second iron around the rim until you've released one side of the tire. Then reach in and remove the inner tube.

5. Inflate the tube with a pump and check it for leaks, marking it the way you did before.

6. Release the air from the tube. Then, following the instructions in your patch kit, apply the patch over the hole and reinflate the tire. Check to make sure the leak is closed, and that there isn't another one.

7. Examine the inside of the casing. *Very carefully*, run your fingers over the tire's inside. Keep a light touch in case there's a nail or some glass lodged in there. Ferret out any foreign objects, and check for any breaks or cuts that might pinch the tubes. If you find a break one-quarter inch or longer, resign yourself to only temporary repairs. Replace the tire or have it checked professionally as soon as possible.

8. Next, work one side of the tire casing onto the rim with your fingers. Place the tube inside the casing, inflating it just enough to give it some shape. Smooth the tube in gently, releasing air from it if necessary. If you have high-pressure clinchers, you might have to work the last section of the tube on with a tire iron. You may well be sick and tired of the whole procedure by now, and you could risk shredding the tube with the iron. This might send you completely berserk, so keep reminding yourself that you are almost home free.

9. Replace the wheel in the frame and inflate it to normal pressure. Reengage the brake's quick release, tighten the axle nut, and off you go.

This procedure takes some time, and ace cyclist John Marino advises carrying spare tubes instead of a patch kit on the road. Then all you have to do is remove the punctured tube, check the casing, and reassemble the whole. The spare tube can fold up to be the same size as a sew-up, giving you sew-up convenience at a clincher price. Bill Bryant also recommends CO_2 tire inflators (Qwik-Fil is one brand name), which will fill your tires in 2 seconds flat, if you'll pardon the expression. These inflators are inexpensive. "Besides," says Bryant, "your arms may be tired from swimming, and these inflators save you energy as well as time."

A lot of technique ... and maybe some innovation

Cycling technique operates on the same aerodynamic principles as a sports car. The more exposed surfaces that leap out in the face of wind resistance, the slower your progress. Streamlining involves tucking in as many of those air-catchers as you can. Until recently most authorities have been fierce on the subject, insisting that there is one correct position for everyone. Don't be afraid to find the riding style that works best for you. You don't want to ruin a perfectly decent weekend jaunt to the mountains by acting as if you're about to be shot out of a cannon. Simply acting as a juggernaut that crashes into as few air molecules as possible will do.

Herewith some streamlining pointers:

1. *Slouch!* Yes—round your shoulders, assume bad posture, look like a vulture, say Audrey McElmury and Michael Levonas, authors of *Bicycle Training for the Triathlete*. "This is not very good for your running technique," they warn, "so you might want to compromise by standing up straight at all other times." On the other hand, this may be your one opportunity for revenge against that creepy aunt who was always digging her fist into the middle of your back to make you straighten up for those endless extended-family photo sessions.

2. Keep changing your head position. The cycling life is tough enough without constricting the flow of blood to your brain.

3. Novices tend to keep their elbows straight while on a bicycle. Don't. Bent elbows are better shock absorbers. Bend them, tuck them in, and drop your hands comfortably to the handlebars. Don't hold them in a death grip.

4. Stay low, trying to keep at least a 45-degree bend in your torso.

5. Keep your knees in and legs relaxed for the least amount of muscle stress, with the ball of each foot centered over the pedal axle. This will force your upper body into a correct but comfortable position.

6. Try to keep those bent elbows tucked even when you get tired. Letting them flap in the breeze is like trying to ice skate in coat and tails.

7. *What to do with the hands.* Although keeping hands in the drops (lowest position on handlebars) promotes the most streamlined position, even hardcore racers can only manage that half the time. On long, flat stretches, let your hands rest on the top of the handlebars—not much streamlining, but a better way of taking in the whitecaps in the ocean to your left and the sweep of the mountains to your right. Slide onto the brake hoods and tuck back down if someone's gaining on you. Streamlining by staying tucked every living minute is important in a short race, but try to keep comfortable in a longer siege.

8. Put your energy into your legs. Don't strain your arms by leaning too far forward, as if you're trying to push yourself ahead, especially if your arms are crying for mercy after a swim. Pushing too much weight forward will force you to work harder than would benefit a long effort. *Remember that energy efficiency and long endurance are your cross-training aims.*   .

Toe clips:
Thinking in circles

Divide pedaling into the *power* or *downstroke*, which begins with the leg at the 12 o'clock position, and the *upstroke*, which takes over from 6 o'clock back up to 12. The 8 to 12 o'clock portion of the upstroke is about as rough as the follow-through part of your freestyle stroke. Because of the angle of your body over the pedals and the relatively greater strength of your quadriceps to your hamstrings in that position, the upstroke will feel awkward at first. This is where many novices make the mistake of resting and riding the impetus back. "Cycling power only comes when you consciously *lift* here. Press those muscles into service," says Marc Thompson.

To make a cross-training point of comparison, figure that it might take you about 700 arm-recovery strokes to cover a mile in the pool. "But if you're riding 100 miles in 6 hours at a comfortable 16.6 miles per hour," says ultramarathon cyclist Michael Shermer, "you're averaging 60 revolutions per minute of the cranks. That means 21,600 circles with each leg over that distance!" Not to belittle the importance of the power phase of your swimming stroke, but that similar call to arms during cycling can have more astounding energy-conservation effects in a sports-combined, long-endurance effort.

You might have been hoping we'd leave those damn toe clips in an accessory rundown. But they have reared their ugly heads once again. They are the ball and chain of the neophyte cross-trainer, but trust me just this once. Properly adjusted, they will allow you to exert more force throughout the pedaling revolution than you would otherwise have, and they'll get you through that 8 to 12 o'clock part with the sort of energy conservation that should be your staple as a triathlete. With toe clips, as Shermer says, you can pull back and up for the upstroke, and press forward and down for the downstroke, without worrying about slipping off the pedals. All that would be impossible without them.

Now that I've made a case for them, be aware that toe clips that are too long allow your foot to slip too far forward, injuring your instep and reducing your pedaling efficiency. A too-short toe clip will cause tendinitis in your Achilles tendon.

Bill Bryant, among many others, recommends smooth-bottomed cycling shoes to beginners because they're easier to release from the stranglehold of toe clips. Their lesser grip on the pedals will make you confident about pulling your foot out whenever you want, the way you need to hover close to the shoreline just beyond the surf when you start open-water swimming. If you need to loosen the strap, wait for the high-noon position so you don't have to reach down too far.

When you are advanced enough to require cleats, practice releasing the straps entirely. Lean down and flip the quick-release buckle on the strap to liberate your foot. When you reach this point, you'll be experienced enough to master the move without too many qualms.

Pacing... a matter of combating what the terrain throws you

To boil a lot of jargon down to simple talk, *pedaling cadence* is the speed at which you turn the pedals. That ends up in a certain number of pedal revolutions per minute (called rpm). If your pedal cadence is 90 rpm, each leg is hitting the 12 o'clock position 90 times in a minute. You could count the revolutions, of course, but why bother when a perfectly decent cycling computer can simply flash the numbers in your face? When you know from experience what a certain cadence feels like in a given gear on a specified terrain, let instincts instead of numbers be your guide.

Don't make the beginner's mistake of putting your bicycle into a high gear (fewer rpm) and slowly grinding against the pedals, thinking that you're getting better exercise. Cross-trainers must be ever vigilant in their pursuit of energy shortcuts. Your bicycle will move farther on one turn of the pedal in high gear, but the you-don't-get-something-for-nothing maxim immediately applies. It's much more of an energy drain.

Stick to *spinning* in a pedal cadence between 75–90. "Less than 75 and you're asking for knee problems," says Bryant. "More than 90 and you're wasting energy." Even though professional racers get up to 120 rpm, you won't be efficient at that level. For endurance work, you want to adjust your gears so that your exertion and pedal cadence remain relatively constant despite hill and dale.

Gearing:
Smooth maintenance of pedal cadence

Your derailleured bicycle has eight or more gears in between its high and low extremes so that you always have a combination suitable for any riding condition. Ask your shop expert and coach to explain *gearing, shifting,* and *gear ratios* to you, and ask to see a gear-ratio chart.

Each gear you shift into on your bicycle, as determined by the number of teeth on the front and back cogs being used at the time, allows you to travel a certain number of inches per pedal revolution. (The number of inches is figured by multiplying a gear-ratio chart's lineup of all possible back-and-front cog configurations you can shift into, times 3.14, or pi—the wheel's diameter.)

Because everyone's bike has a different number of teeth per cog, it's easier for a coach to yell out that everyone should be in an 84-inch gear, for instance, than to bellow, "You get in a 50 × 16 gear; you get in 53 × 17; you get in a 44 × 14," and so on. In the case of the 50 × 16, 50 represents the number of teeth on the front chainwheel and 16 the number on one of the back cogs.

This is the sort of explanation that sounds impossibly confusing on paper, particularly if mathematics is the bane of your existence. Don't worry about all of this. One demonstration from your coach is worth a thousand words here.

Developing gearing instincts

1. Beginners give themselves away every time because they ride in too-high gears. As fast as they seem to be cruising, they're wasting the energy they'll want to direct into running when they hop off their bikes.

2. Conserve cross-training energy by breathing from your diaphragm. Novices often fall under the spell of breathing-per-pedal-stroke.

3. *Anticipation* will save you time in developing your gearing instincts. You want to hit a hill or curve in the right gear, *not adjust when you're in the thick of it*. Don't be afraid to subject your bicycle to a reasonable amount of learner's wear and tear.

4. *Shifting* requires predicting what's about to happen. Don't wait until you are huffing and puffing up a hill—shift to a lower gear when you see the hill looming on the horizon.

5. *Shift before corners, brake before turns*. Your brakes and body will thank you. Avoid shifting when pushing hard on the pedals, which puts undue strain on the derailleur. Instead, gear yourself into a constant cadence over your chosen terrain so that you're working in your target aerobic heart range. Anticipate anything the road throws you so that you can always stay between 75–90 rpm.

6. "When you're about to round a corner, put pressure on the outside pedal and get the center of gravity as low as possible," says Marc Thompson. "Look the curve over before you get there so you can set up your line. Visualize a curved line, and stay on it."

7. When it comes to hills, Bob Curtis recommends getting out of the saddle for two or three strokes at a time to aid your circulation and to maintain your rpm level. When you're more experienced, you'll be able to take most of it sitting down. Use a low gear for hills, shifting prior to arrival, or for headwinds or situations that make pedaling difficult. Switch to a higher gear for downhills, tailwinds, or level ground.

8. Remember that most accidents to beginners occur because the cyclers are overly timid, not because they're reckless.

Wind-load simulators

Finally! Wind-load simulators may just be the best invention for multisport aficionados ever to come down the pike. Back in 1978,

Wilfried Baatz, a West German–born mechanical engineer busily producing gasoline flow meters at his Seattle company, was determined to fit some avid cycling into his busy schedule. Thus the wind-load simulator was born. Many variations of Baatz's original Racer-Mate now exist, but basically your bicycle is set on a stand with a wheel-and-blower-fan assembly either on top of or under your rear tire. The motion of your rear wheel then drives the blower-fan assembly, which draws in air and redistributes it to simulate the wind resistance you'd feel on the road. You can practice shifting and pedal cadence to your heart's content without worrying about dogs, glass shards, sleet, skateboarders, or Buicks at any time of the day or night.

Safety

1. Return home at once and put on the helmet.
2. Obey all rules of the road. You may be ticketed as readily as a. motor vehicle.
3. Don't expect motorists to see you. Wear bright clothing and use reflector tape.

JOSH MITCHELL

A wind-load simulator allows a cyclist to continue training and work on technique when nightfall, winter, or a shortage of time interferes. There are even treadmill-system swimming cabinets and runner's treadmills for the all-around indoor triathlete.

4. Be prepared. Fred Matheny reports that he once "almost got cooked by a goose" while cycling, and on another occasion he rounded a corner and came eyeball to eyeball with a full-grown male buffalo. Dogs are more mundane but omnipresent. No amount of reflective tape will keep an angry dog at bay. Keep the dog away from your front wheel to prevent cyclical somersaults. Frighten it away by yelling, raising your hand, and pretending to throw something at it.

5. Ride defensively. Remember that your fellow bipeds, color-fully attired though they may be, can be as big a nuisance as their canine counterparts. If you are in the front of a pack, point out road hazards, but don't waste time yelling back blow-by-blow descriptions of the offending items. No one will hear you anyway. Let loose some all-purpose holler, and don't take your eyes off the road for a second.

6. When you come to railroad tracks, slow down, get out of the saddle, and use the handlebars to lift yourself and your bike over the tracks. Don't try to jump them, but keep yourself up to lessen the pressure on impact and to reduce tire or rim damage.

Once you're more of an old hand, borrow an older bicycle, preferably from someone you're mad at, and practice jumping in a smooth, grassy area. Fred Matheny suggests pulling up evenly on the drop part of the handlebars and simultaneously pulling up on the pedals. If you're lucky, E.T. will be in the neighborhood and make it easy for you.

7. The joys of cycling include navigating slippery or loose-gravel roads. Always bank carefully, especially in lousy weather or in a rural area, because a buffalo may be awaiting you on the other side. In the event of a skid, keep your weight toward the rear of the bicycle and sit back in the seat. Avoid abrupt moves, and let your bicycle find its own way out of the mess it's gotten you into. When you come to gravel, sit back and try to get through it by hitting a higher gear and maintaining a light touch on the bike.

8. Leave the headphones at home.

Stretching

Bob Anderson gives an abbreviated but thorough stretching plan for cross-trainers ready to start a workout with cycling.

Cycling Stretches

1. To stretch the upper hamstrings and hip, hold on to the outside of your ankle with one hand, with your other hand and forearm around your bent knee. Gently pull the leg as one unit toward your chest until you feel an easy stretch in the back of the upper leg. You may want to do this stretch while you rest your back against something for support. Hold for 30 seconds. Make sure the leg is pulled as one unit so that no stress is felt in the knee. Do both legs.

2. Sit with your right leg bent, with your right heel just to the outside of your right hip. The left leg is bent, and the sole of your left foot is next to the inside of your upper right leg. (Try not to let your right foot flare out to the side in this position.) Now slowly lean straight back until you feel an easy stretch in your right quadriceps. Use hands for balance and support. Hold an easy stretch for 30 seconds. Do not hold any stretches that are painful to the knee. Do both legs.

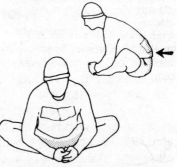

3. After stretching your quads, practice tightening the buttocks on the side of the bent leg as you turn the hip over. This will help stretch the front of your hip and give a better overall stretch to the upper-thigh area. After contracting the butt muscles for 5–8 seconds, let the buttock relax. Then continue to stretch quads for another 15 seconds. Do both legs.

4. Put the soles of your feet together with your heels a comfortable distance from your groin. Now put your hands around your feet and slowly pull yourself forward until you feel an easy stretch in the groin. Make your movement forward by bending from the hips and not from the shoulders. If possible, keep your elbows on the outside of your lower legs for greater stability during the stretch. Hold a comfortable stretch for 30–40 seconds.

5. Sit with your right leg straight. Bend your left leg, cross your left foot over, and rest it to the outside of your right knee. Then bend your right elbow and rest it on the outside of your upper left thigh, just above the knee. During the stretch use the elbow to keep this leg stationary with controlled pressure to the inside. Now, with your left hand resting behind you, slowly turn your head to look over your left shoulder, and at the same time rotate your upper body toward your left hand and arm. As you turn your upper body, think of turning your hips in the same direction (though your hips won't move because your right elbow is keeping the left leg stationary). This should give you a stretch in your lower back and side of hip. Hold for 15 seconds. Do both sides. Don't hold your breath; breathe easily.

6. Interlace your fingers behind your head and rest your arms on the mat. Using the power of your arms, **slowly** bring your head, neck, and shoulders forward until you feel a slight stretch. Hold an easy stretch for 5 seconds. Repeat three times. Do not overstretch.

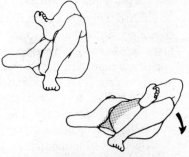

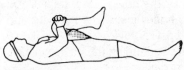

7. Next, straighten both legs and relax, then pull your left leg toward your chest. For this stretch keep the back of your head on the mat, if possible, but don't strain. Hold an easy stretch for 30 seconds. Repeat, pulling your right leg toward your chest.

8. From a bent knee position, interlace your fingers behind your head and lift the left leg over the right leg. From here, use your left leg to pull your right leg toward the floor until you feel a stretch along the side of your hip and lower back. Stretch and relax. Keep the upper back, shoulders, and elbows flat on the floor. The idea is not to touch the floor with your right knee, but to stretch within your limits. Hold for 30 seconds. Repeat stretch for other side.

To complement the cycling routine, use the upper-body stretches from the swimming routine.

CREDIT: BOB ANDERSON
ILLUSTRATIONS BY JEAN ANDERSON

The long and winding roads

First, invest in over-distance training, and plenty of it. Some coaches recommend at least 800 road miles before beginning interval work, while Fred Matheny sets the qualifying numbers at 1000–1500 steady miles in low gear. Once again, train for time, not distance. Because of variable road conditions, it's harder than ever to judge the impact of mileage, particularly when talking about a novice who is becoming more adroit at shifting and the nuances of gearing.

LSD cycling is your prime cross-training chance to learn what it takes, mentally and physically, to handle endurance work—the stuff that can make or break all your triathloning goals. Kathleen McCartney put it in perspective during the 1982 Davis Double Century race. She found herself with only 10 miles left after riding for 9 hours. She was in second place, and at that point detoured to follow an arrow leading to a restroom. She then discovered she was on the same street as her hotel.

"I'd had enough by then," she said. "I went to my room, showered, and returned to the finish line. It turned out that the first place woman had dropped out, and I would have won. More important than that, my friends had already finished and were waiting for me, and I suddenly became very disappointed that I hadn't finished too. I felt so bad I went back to my room, changed, and finished the ride.

"I think that a good 200-mile bike ride is one of the best introductions to ultraendurance for the novice cross-trainer. You learn what it's like to spend 9–15 hours in sustained activity, and how you react to it physically and psychologically. And, unlike 10 hours of running or swimming, it's something the novice can do without being devastated the next day."

Give yourself confidence when embarking on a long ride by using a checklist compiled by Michael Shermer through years of sometimes costly trial and error.

Essential Items for any Ride

☐ Spare tube or sew-up tire (rim glue or rim tape if using sew-ups)

☐ Patch kit—complete

☐ 1 water bottle—filled

☐ Tools: spoke wrench, tire irons,

Allen wrenches or open-end wrenches, screwdriver
- [ ] Helmet
- [ ] Money

Personal items:

_____

_____

_____

_____

Add the following, according to riding conditions:

Hot Weather
- [ ] Sunglasses
- [ ] Sunscreen or block
- [ ] Two or more water bottles (you can put one in the back pocket of your jersey)
- [ ] ERG or an electrolyte replacement drink
- [ ] Scarf or handkerchief to protect the back of your neck from the heat

Cold Weather
- [ ] Leg warmers
- [ ] Arm warmers
- [ ] Wool jersey
- [ ] Wool warm-up jacket
- [ ] Shoe covers to keep feet warm
- [ ] Long-fingered gloves or glove liners
- [ ] Bike cap under helmet
- [ ] Windbreaker
- [ ] Handkerchief or scarf for neck or nose

Night Riding
- [ ] Bike lights: front and rear
- [ ] Reflective tape on bike and clothes and helmet
- [ ] Reflective vest
- [ ] Small flashlight for map review, tire patching, etc.

Rain Riding
- [ ] Booties
- [ ] Fenders on bike, if available
- [ ] All clothes should be wool (stays warm even when wet)
- [ ] Eye protection (clear goggles)
- [ ] Extra socks

50- to 100-Mile Ride
- [ ] 2 water bottles
- [ ] Food in jersey pockets or in handlebar/frame bag
- [ ] A change of clothes if it is an overnight trip
- [ ] Bike computer, if desired (a great motivator on long rides)

100- to 150-Mile Ride or beyond
- [ ] 3 water bottles, unless there are plenty of services along the course
- [ ] Extra money and/or credit card
- [ ] Moist towelettes to clean up during a break or when finished
- [ ] Maps of the course
- [ ] Night riding gear in case you get caught in the dark
- [ ] Extra food—as much as you can carry in case stores are closed
- [ ] A granola bar or an apple to save through the entire trip. If you bonk with no help in sight, it can help tide you over.
- [ ] Extra socks

The aerobic stress plateau

1. Avoid knee injury by selecting a gear that allows you to maintain 75–90 rpm while keeping your heart rate within its target stress-base range.

2. Pedal along for at least 20 minutes per session when you first start out.

3. If your heart rate exceeds the proper range, select the next lowest gear, and continue pedaling at 75–90 rpm.

4. If your heart rate is below what it should be, select the next highest gear. Don't forget to warm up and cool down.

The following sample aerobic workout can be done on your wind-load simulator.

Aerobic Workout

Warm-up	Aerobic training	Warm-down
5 minutes in a 42 × 18 gear (63″)	20 minutes (light workout), 30–35 minutes (moderate workout), 60 minutes (to peak for races)	5 minutes in a 42 × 18 gear (63″)

Suggested gearing: Pedal at 90–100 rpm in a 52 × 18, 19, or 20, depending on fitness level

---

CREDIT: REPRINTED WITH PERMISSION OF BARCLAY KRUSE.

A word about drafting

A triathlon is a race against the clock, as well as against other competitors. Although you want to conserve energy, and you won't be penalized for swimming in someone else's wake, expect to be disqualified and generally excoriated for drafting (conserving energy by riding in another's slipstream) in the cycling leg of a triathlon.

Practice riding alone often enough so that you do not become physically or mentally dependent on drafting. "Besides," says Jennifer Hinshaw, "riding solo forces you to face situations you might encounter on race day." If there are always more knowledgeable mechanics in your midst, they'll always want to repair your flat tires so that the pack can move apace.

Intervals—preparation for time trials

Always lengthen your warm-up cycling to at least 10–15 minutes before every interval session. After that, select the highest gear that will allow you to sprint at your maximum pedal cadence. On a wind-load simulator, you want to pedal your rear wheel at the highest possible speed. That takes some experimenting, but you'll get better as your cycling improves.

If at any point you can't maintain this top pedaling speed for the full interval session, stop. Note how many you could do, and go into your cool-down. That gives you your goal the next time around—to do at least one more interval than you could manage this time.

When you can do a string of 10 interval sprints in one workout at top speed, increase your gearing and start the learning process over again. Whenever you can't match a previous achievement, switch to more LSD work or complete rest, and don't discount the crossover effect interval work in other sports will have on your cycling.

Anaerobic Workout

Warm-up	Anaerobic training	Warm-down
10–15 minutes in a 42 × 18 gear (63″)	60-seconds full-speed interval, 60-seconds rest interval (90 rpm); repeat 10 times	10–15 minutes in a 42 × 18 gear (63″)

Suggested gearing: Hard interval: 52 × 18 to 13, depending on fitness level; rest interval: 52 × 21

Everyone has a different idea about how much cycling interval work a novice cross-trainer with an established aerobic base should attempt. Scott Molina does speedwork twice a week, but Matheny warns that beginners should hold themselves to one session a week. After your race, *back off*. Return to aerobic workouts, and begin the climb again, trying for higher-quality exercise than your first go-around. As we'll see in Chapter 7, being able to do anaerobic work doesn't mean that you shouldn't shelve it at different times of the year and cling to aerobics. *It's the year's overview that will help you make the most of your fitness.*

More cycling interval options:

1. *Fartlek training.* Marc Thompson recommends 1 minute fast, 1 minute slow. Try 20–30 per workout.

2. *Hour-record intervals.* Try racing as fast as you can (103–108 rpm) for 1 hour. Record your distances to chart your improvement.

3. *Race-conscious fartlek work.* Audrey McElmury and Michael Levonas prescribe intervals according to your race or goal distance:

> If the bike leg of your triathlon is 25 miles or less, do 1 minute on, 1 minute off (meaning easy riding).

> If the cycling segment is about 50 miles, try 2–3 minutes on, 2 minutes off.

> If it's 100 miles or more, do 5-minute intervals with 2½ minutes rest.

Teach yourself pacing by not going all-out on the first interval of each session. You want to maintain the same speed and intensity until the end.

4. *Tempo training.* High gear, low-gear—push one, spin one, going 10 minutes on and 5 minutes off. Try 20–30 per ride. Slowly increase gears, with higher gears each tempo session. This is a good way to learn gearing.

5. *Time trials.* Design your own "track" and assess your progress in preparation for an organized time trial. Many bike clubs and shops hold them regularly, or you can write to the U.S. Cycling Federation (USCF) at 1750 East Boulder, Colorado Springs, CO 80909 (303 632-5551), for information about the trials in your area. USCF sponsors 25-mile trials in every district in the country, but enter one only after you've been through many dry runs on your home-designed course.

Confine those first trials to 5–10-mile bursts over flat terrain. Choose a course free of cross-traffic, and write down your times. You should be feeling stronger and wiser—not more tired—as you improve.

After you've developed a smooth pedal cadence of 80–90 rpm at your aerobic threshold, add hills and move into a higher gear. "Time trialing breaks up the lazy, uninspired patterns of everyday distance training," says former Olympic cyclist John Howard.

As your progress becomes more apparent, you'll develop an appetite for speedwork. Despite the somewhat ominous overload of numbers and mechanical dictums offered here and in cycling-training manuals, your cross-training goal should be to pursue precision only insofar as it gives you direct contact with the joys of the open road. Cycling can then be a key to sharpening your fitness course.

Manuals

Michael B. Shermer
  Psychling
  Melton Printing, Hollywood, CA (213 465-3501), 1982
John Marino, Lawrence May, and Hal Z. Bennett
  John Marino's Bicycling Book
Ed Burke (ed.)
  Velo-News, Inside the Cyclist
  Brattleboro, VT, 1981
Marcia Holoman, et. al. (eds.)
  (Bicycling), The Most Frequently Asked Questions About Bicycling
  Rodale Press, Emmaus, PA,
  Excellent for beginners
Fred Matheny
  Beginning Bicycle Racing
  Velo-News, Brattleboro, VT 1981
Jack Simes
  Winning Bicycle Racing
  Contemporary Books, Chicago, 1976
  Endorsed by the U.S. Cycling Federation
Eugene A. Sloane
  Bicycle Maintenance Manual
  (also author of the bestselling *The Complete Book of Bicycling* and *The New, Complete Book of Bicycling*)
Michael J. Kolin and Denise M. de la Rosa
  The Custom Bicycle
  Rodale Press, Emmaus, PA, 1979
Audrey McElmury and Michael Levonas
  Bicycle Training for the Triathlete
  Iris Press, 308 A Street, Encinitas, CA 92024

Periodicals

Bicycle Sport
  Wizard Publications
  3162 Kashiwa St.
  Torrance, CA 90505
  (213) 539-9213
Bicycling
  Rodale Press
  33 E. Minor St.
  Emmaus, PA 18049
  (215) 967-5171

Velo-News
  Box 1257
  Brattleboro, VT 05301-1257
  (802) 254-2305
Journal of bicycle racing
Cycling USA
  1750 E. Boulder
  Colorado Springs, CO 80909
For members of the United States Cycling Federation only

Organizations

U.S. Cycling Federation
  1750 East Boulder
  Colorado Springs, CO 80909
  (303) 632-5551
For information on time trials in your area

TRANSITION 2

Let thy attire be comely, but not costly.
                                —John Lyly (1554–1606),
                                    Euphues: The Anatomy of Wit

Bike-to-run

Triathlete Dave Horning, winner of the 1982 Swim Around Manhattan, wore a skin-fitting one-piece ensemble throughout the 1981 Ironman. It looked weird—but changed the style of an entire sport. It was an aerodynamically sound body stocking that minimized drag in the water, prevented chafing during cycling, and deflected sunburn in the run. Horning's tri-suit (also called a skin suit) was a brazen handling of cross-training's unique segue from sport to sport, without so much as a change of costume to acknowledge a break in the action.

Instead of a three-sport consciousness requiring different outfits, skin suits promote a sense of triathloning as one continuous effort. They're yet another energy saver, and a stylish one at that. Look for skin suits with colorful Hawaiian sunsets, new-wave geometry, and polka dots the next time you're at the races.

Physiologically speaking

Just as Djan Madruga began mock-cycling in the water prior to entering the first transition, *start running on your bicycle* before you dismount. Don't think that just because cycling strength comes

Julie Lilly, in a Hawaiian sunset suit, tests the chilly water and early-morning fog that greeted all entrants at the April 9, 1983, USTS Los Angeles triathlon in Bonelli Park.

SHARRI HOGAN

New-wave design worn by Larry Eyler was a standout on the beach before the start of the USTS Los Angeles triathlon.

MARK GORDON/PREFERRED STOCK

from your legs you can bound off your bicycle and run up the road. You've shortened your quadriceps, the acting agonists during cycling, which will make your running unsteady for at least the first half-mile. The blood pooled in your quadriceps must be *gradually* redirected to the backs of your legs.

To lessen the probability of wobbling around in the all-too-familiar dance step of bike-to-run syndrome, thereby burning out your running energies too quickly, Dave Scott recommends planning your transition, whether you're training or racing, during the last few miles of your ride—not merely as an afterthought at the end.

1. First, stretch your calves, Achilles tendons, hip flexors, and lower back by standing up on your bicycle as if you were climbing a hill. Drop your lower foot down with the heel below the pedal, and lean forward slightly, keeping your lower leg fairly straight. Repeat with the other leg.

2. Also, try backpedaling for 10–15 revolutions, dropping your heel down at the bottom of each stroke. To initiate the hip stretch while on the bike, stand up in the same position as the previous stretch, and push your hips toward the stem. Upon dismounting your bike, take your cycling shoes off and walk backward 15–25 yards, then walk forward, gradually increasing your stride.

3. Spin slowly the last 2 to ½ miles (50–70 rpm) in a low gear, concentrating on relaxing your legs, ankles, and feet. Release your toe clips.

4. During the transition, try to regain a comfortable breathing pattern, letting your stomach expand and contract. This will relax your tense shoulders, arms, and back. Do not force your breathing by elevating your chest.

5. During the first half of your run, your steps should be short with a gradual lengthening to your normal stride gait. Remember to relax your arms and face and *build up* your speed over the next 2–3 miles.

6. These exercises should supplement the static stretches you should do with your entire body before you run. Remember that your upper body, including your arms and shoulders, has been in a relatively rigid and fixed position while you were cycling, and a relaxed and stretched upper body will increase efficiency during the run.

Other transition tips

• "Don't worry about a fast transition your first couple of races," says Julie Moss, who often stays in her swimsuit for an entire short-length triathlon.

• "Begin all transitions before you get there. Don't be concerned if other people pass you when you slow down—a lot of them are burning themselves out too fast," says Bob Curtis.

• "Don't speed in and out of transitions," says Dave Horning. "Relax with them."

• "The first couple of steps will feel funny, but warm into it. It'll get easier," says Mark Allen.

• "Take Dramamine during the swim to prevent seasickness, and extrastrength Tylenol works for general muscular aches and pains," says Richard Marks.

• "Practice changing from your cycling shoes into your running shoes during your training," says Kathleen McCartney.

• Kudos for inventiveness go to Conrad Will for this gem: "Put ice cubes in your cycling cap and wear it during the run. That way you can keep a cool head as the melting ice drizzles the whole way."

• "Don't believe your eyes when you're a tired cyclist," says Bob Curtis. "You'll be seeing too many optical illusions. Listen to your *legs*. They'll tell you if it's a hill or not."

He may well win the race that runs by himself.
—Benjamin Franklin (1706–1790)
Poor Richard's Almanac (1757)

It was entirely coal, my first running trophy. They said it made me the fastest woman in West Virginia, and after that I entered a cycling centennial race to make myself go even faster and farther. That was back in 1977.

I still want to be faster. To do that when I run I never look at the ground. I pick a landmark like the Golden Gate Bridge and see myself crossing it before I get there. That produces a wonderful, floating sensation. I think of great runners—they don't spend much time on the ground.

My brain filters out negative thoughts . . . "I can't do this," or, "This workout doesn't count." I substitute affirmations instead by thinking of myself as a sailplane gliding or a thoroughbred galloping. At first it feels fake, but then you settle into it and you're really flying.

I liked doing somersaults as a child, and I think it took the fear of falling and injury out of me. Of course, one time during an ultradistance triathlon I looked down and saw blood gushing from my shoes. I couldn't feel it. I don't want to run into that kind of trouble too often, but it shows the powerful hold the running state can have over you.

—JoAnn Dahlkoetter, 30,
San Francisco
Sports psychology consultant

CHAPTER 6

Running: Accessibility and simplicity in action

Inventions led to some of the most entertaining stories to come out of last decade's running boom. Look no further than the case of Bill Bowerman, author of the classic book *Jogging* in the early 1960s, track coach of the University of Oregon in its heyday, and champion of jogging for fitness when it was still a fleeting eccentricity. Bowerman was also one of Nike's 17 founding fathers, which brings us to the tale of how Bowerman created the waffle-soled running shoe.

"One day I saw some workers pouring urethane track," says Bill, "and I got an idea. I asked if I could mix and pour some myself, one pint at a time. They said okay and showed me how.

"The next Sunday, while my wife was at church, I poured a pint of urethane into her waffle iron. I was rushing to get it done before she got home, and I forgot to put in the releasing agent. I had to act fast. I tried to pull the urethane out with some pliers, but it wouldn't budge. I threw the whole mess into the oven and tried to burn it out. When it was red hot, I managed to tear it out of the iron, but by then it was limp and just leaned over the table. It was a mess, but I knew exactly what I wanted."

Though she was not hankering for a waffle at the time, Bowerman's wife was upset upon her return from church. "First I bought her a new one," says Bill. "Then I visited every secondhand shop in Eugene and collected every old waffle iron I got my hands on. After pouring urethane into 40 or 50 of them, I finally got it right." The waffle shoe was born to bring sounder running traction to all.

It's emblematic of the abiding and often homespun affection that running inspires. Fitness runners can even afford to be a touch sentimental, considering that their passion is really what gave momentum to the amateur fitness movement—with some help from Kenneth Cooper's *Aerobics* and James Fixx's *Complete Book of Running*. Some say there are now 60 million devotees in the United States alone, while others are adamant that only 40 million qualify as "serious."

If you're one of those 60 million (okay, 40 million)

• Running controls weight better than swimming or cycling because it burns body fat the most effectively.

• Because runners must adapt to rapid heat dissipation (the thermal conductivity of air is 20 times less than that of water), running is the best cross-training sport for toughening the body's thermoregulatory systems.

• Freedom! "Running can be done at any time, in almost any weather, with little equipment investment," says Brian J. Sharkey, author of *Physiology of Fitness* (Human Kinetics Publishers, 1979). "It's possible at any stage of life." No scheduling yourself around pool hours, no bicycle maintenance. It's also the perfect recourse for the fitness-conscious traveler.

• Running is simplicity in action. Swimming mechanics were once developed as a military skill and cycling depends on a machine, but running is natural to the point of being atavistic.

Some reasons for considering a curtailed running agenda

• The stress to your musculoskeletal system has been re-counted many times in this book because running injuries are perhaps the major reason for the advent of cross-training.

• Running has a long recovery rate and therefore requires more subsequent rest time in both the long and short term than swimming or cycling.

Anne Dandoy and
Mark Montgom-
ery at USTS race.

BUD LIGHT UNITED STATES TRIATHLON SERIES

Equipment

Shoes: Arming (or footing) yourself for action requires finding a specialty shop that offers well-padded, flexible shoes with stable heels. You want the shoe's rear to land first the better to absorb most of your body weight as you strike the pavement. This elevated, padded heel also minimizes stretching of the Achilles tendon—a particular selling point to women who've been trooping around in high heels all day. "People who land heavily need more cushioning," says triathlete Sue Kinsey. "After that, the shoe you select is a matter of individual preference."

Try a pair on and parade around the store. They should fit

snugly around the heel and foot's midsection. Wiggle your toes, and make sure that you could ease a finger between the end of your foot and the end of the shoe. Stick to name brands, and expect to pay upwards of $40. The penalty for shoe skimping is sore feet, blisters, and a mere slip of a sole cushion that can cause knee, hip, and back problems later.

That's all, folks. Everything else you'll need is probably already in your closet. Depending on whose advice you take, you can even forgo socks (sockless-but-shoed feet adorn the covers of Jim Fixx's books). Some doctors claim that's declaring open season on blisters and athlete's foot, and pragmatic runners argue that socks prolong the shoe's life. If you must be besocked, at least avoid nylon, which alternately tears and suffocates your feet.

Jogging suits: "Who needs frills?" snorts Scott Molina at the thought of spending a small fortune on a fashionable jogging suit. Nylon running shorts and a T-shirt are serviceable, if not always snazzy. Wear as little as you can get away feeling comfortable with. Fixx dashes that old wives' tale about catching one's death of cold in cold weather by maintaining that you are better off warming up while slightly chilly and then hitting your stride without premature overheating brought on by too many layers of clothing. Brisk weather won't make you sick if you're healthy, but for the genuine cold or rainy seasons, break out the warm-up suits. They're more expensive but lighter and more comfortable than traditional sweatpants. Don't forget a plain wool cap either, because 40 percent of your body heat dissipates through the head. And breathes there a more creative runner than Fixx? He suggest those $1-per-pair white cotton gardener's gloves to keep your hands warm.

Running form as a refuge from fatigue

The running form you find the most comfortable is exactly what's best. That's because your body has its own gravity center, plus its own methods for compensating for it. Unlike cycling or swimming, running is an unfettered natural impulse—think of all that wild game or those fellow nomads our distant ancestors were constantly either pursuing or being pursued by. Land your footstrikes by derivative instinct.

Julie Moss at
USTS races.

SPEEDO. **BUD LIGHT** MIZU
RUNNING SHOE

LIGHT U.S. TRIATHLON S

BUD LIGHT UNITED STATES TRIATHLON SERIES

But when you're tired, some semblance of running form may be all you have to hang your dwindling energies on. It's easy to disintegrate into a shuffling gait that becomes a vicious cycle by making running even more draining, particularly if you've already been swimming and bicycling.

A smooth form enables you to run faster toward the end of a triathlon, and it can prevent injuries by decreasing the amount of shock to your joints and tendons. Besides, being more comfortable not only enhances your enjoyment of running, it sustains you in your fatigued time of need.

Rely on these focal points as mental mantras to help you extend your energies.

1. *Stand up straight.* "This is an important cross-training adjustment from cycling," says Mark Allen. "When you climb off the bike, you tend to hunch over. Put your head and shoulders up. Concentrate on your arm swing, and keep it loose."

2. *You don't just run with your legs.* "Think *arms* when you're tired," says Carol Hogan. "Don't be afraid to move them. They'll help you to the finish line more than your legs." Refrain from wild arm flailing, which will throw your form off-kilter.

"Move your arm from the shoulder, not from the elbow," says Julie Leach, winner of the October 1982 Ironman. "Swing your arms straight forward, and stabilize your pace and form by using a full backswing. Move your hands past your hips with each stride." For faster surges, pump your arms without tightening your shoulders, neck, or hands. A stiff upper body will sap energy from your legs. Don't hold your arms tightly to your chest or make a fist. That causes tension to reverberate throughout your body.

3. *Heads up!* Don't stare at the ground. Keep your eyes to the horizon, and as you look forward to each passing landmark, pretend that you're reeling it in.

4. *Resist the temptation to sprint "to make up time."* Unless the finish line is a stone's throw and you need to kick into an anaerobic gear to pass someone, keep that steady pace you're confident in. *Let others pass you by.* They may be tiring themselves out so that you can pass them later on. "Keep a lower tempo in cross-training, running slower than you feel you could handle all-out," says triathlete Sue Kinsey. "Speed's less important in a triathlon than *pacing.*"

5. *Land on your heels.* A common beginner's mistake is to strain the Achilles tendon by landing on the toes. Land on your well-cushioned heels, roll forward, and push off with your toes.

6. *Think of good posture.* When you begin to tire in swimming, it's easy to shorten your reach and slap the water with choppy, deadbeat strokes. The upstroke part of cycling becomes a trial. In running, it's tempting to slump and think you'll never escape this misery alive.

Each of those aerobic scenarios can be prolonged by settling into a metronomelike rhythm in which sheer posture can see you through. Mentally cycle through your body to see if you're relaxed. Knowing your limits, however, also means knowing when it's time to throw in the towel.

7. *Wobbling wastes energy.* "Keep the area between your shoulder blades loose to prevent lower-back pain," says Mark Allen. "Keep your head straight so you won't sway around."

8. *Don't overstride.* Overstriding will tighten your hamstrings so that they give out early. Understriding, on the other hand, is uncomfortable and inefficient. Land on your heels. Sprinters run on their toes because they are only traveling a short distance. Sprinters who stride in a long-distance effort the way they think feels "natural" will end up nursing sore calves and Achilles tendinitis.

David Costill and Lawrence Armstrong at the Human Performance Laboratory have observed that sprinters show a more forward lean than marathoners, as well as a longer range of arm motion. The difference is even more striking in stride length. During a marathon, the footstrikes of marathoners are more efficient than the longer, bouncier strides of the sprinters. Marathoners show an average vertical lift of 9 centimeters, sprinters 11. Over 26.2 miles, those 2 extra centimeters add up to a lot of wasted energy and muscle strain. If you're traditionally a sprinter who wants to move into long-distance work or triathlons, have a coach help you rethink your stride.

9. *Don't slap your foot flat on the ground.* "That creates a braking action," says JoAnn Dahlkoetter, "which forces you to waste energy because you must accelerate out of each step. Think of yourself as flying—*floating* over the pavement."

10. "*Remember that running is a delicate sport,*" says Dahlkoetter. "Stay off asphalt, and don't run on the beach. The sand's slant and lack of support puts terrible stress on your knees." Those movie scenes of running on the beach are nice, but it's the sunset the cameras want to capture. They're not trying to demonstrate true running horse sense. Stick as much as possible to soft grass or soft dirt surfaces.

11. *All you must do is simply begin.* "It's not so much *how* you run," says Bill Bowerman, "it's *that* you run. Some of you will never be

very pretty runners. In fact, a lot of Olympic marathoners have terrible posture and beat everybody. Do it, and don't worry about trying to look right."

Pacing... and new running philosophies

Your cardiovascular and respiratory systems are so sharpened from other cross-training sports—and maybe from years of running—that your sports-combined dilemma may not be trying

The Puntous twins working out together.

to run faster, but *trying to run slower*. At the beginning of a long distance, your pace should start out making you feel impatient with yourself. It's the same adjustment a star swimmer must enforce at the start of a triathlon so as not to blow it all barely out of the starting gate.

If this sounds a trifle odd—isn't the point always to go as fast as possible?—it's because now that you're combining running with other sports, your perception of running pace must also change.

1. Running is usually at the end of an official triathlon, which puts "going as fast as you can" into an entirely new frame of reference.

2. The stress of other sports makes garbage mileage in running even more of a waste. Evidence of this new running attitude is everywhere. Middle-distance specialist Mary Decker used to suffer extreme injuries until she cut her mileage back. She now runs as fast as ever. A while back, George Sheehan, M.D., shifted from running six days a week to three, and after a few years of that he managed his best marathon ever (about 2:56) at age 62. Even inveterate runner Ken Cooper recommends limiting weekly mileage for those who simply want to get in condition. Turn to other sports to get your aerobic fix, but especially to circumvent injury.

3. Studies by the German physiologist Woldemar Gerschler disclose that the key to running performance is raising the heart to its maximum performance level and then allowing it enough recovery time so that the heart actually enlarges and thereby extends its pumping capacities. In short: interval work. You must run for time, not distance.

Stretches

Bob Anderson suggests the following stretches before your running and after your cool-down.

Running Stretches

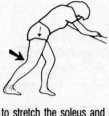

1. To stretch your calf, stand a little way from a solid support and lean on it with your forearms, your head resting on your hands. Bend one leg and place your foot on the ground in front of you, leaving the other leg straight behind you. Slowly move your hips forward until you feel a stretch in the calf of your straight leg. Be sure to keep the heel of the foot of the straight leg on the ground and your toes pointed straight ahead. Hold an easy stretch for 30 seconds. Do not bounce. Stretch both legs.

2. Now, to stretch the soleus and Achilles tendon, slightly bend the back knee, keeping the foot flat. This gives you a much lower stretch, which is also good for maintaining or regaining ankle flexibility. Do 15 seconds for each leg. This area needs only a slight feeling of stretch.

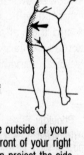

3. Stand a little way from a solid support and lean on it with your forearms, head resting on hands. Bend one leg and place your foot on the ground in front of you, with the other leg straight behind. To stretch the outside of your hip, slightly turn the front of your right hip to the inside. Then project the side of your right hip to the side as you lean your shoulders very slightly in the opposite direction of your hips to create the stretch. Hold an even stretch for 30 seconds. Do both legs. Keep foot of back leg pointed straight ahead with heel flat on ground.

4. Opposite hand to opposite foot—quads and knee stretch. Hold top of left foot (from inside of foot) with right hand and gently pull, heel moving toward buttocks. The knee bends at a natural angle in this position and creates a good stretch in knee and quads. Especially good to do if you have had trouble or feel pain stretching in the hurdle stretch position leaning back, or when pulling the right heel to butt with the right (same) hand. Pulling opposite hand to opposite foot does not create any adverse angles in the knee and is especially good in knee rehab and with problem knees. Hold for 30 seconds. Do both legs.

5. Place the ball of your foot up on a secure support of some kind (wall, fence, table). Keep the down leg pointed straight ahead. Now, bend the knee of the up leg and move your hips forward. This should stretch your groin, hamstrings, and front of hip. Hold for 30 seconds. This stretch will make it easier to lift your knees. If possible, for balance and control, use your hands to hold onto the support. Do both legs.

6. Rest your foot up on something (a fence, table, rock) that is at a comfortable height for you. The leg on the ground should be nearly straight with your foot pointed forward as in a proper walking or running position. The leg resting on the support you are using should be at a comfortable height and straight. Slowly bend forward, until you feel a good stretch in the back of the raised leg. Hold and relax. Find an easy stretch, relax, and then stretch further when it becomes easier to increase the stretch. Hold stretch for 30 seconds for each leg.

7. With your feet shoulder width apart and pointed out to about a 15° angle, heels on the ground, bend your knees and squat down. Your knees should be directly above your big toes. If you have trouble staying in this position, hold onto something for support. It is a great stretch for your ankles, Achilles tendons, groin, lower back and hips. Hold stretch for 30 seconds. Be careful if you have had any knee problems. If pain is present, discontinue this stretch.

8. Shoulder Shrug: Raise the top of your shoulders toward your ears until you feel slight tension in your neck and shoulders. Hold this feeling of tension for 3–5 seconds, then relax your shoulders downward into their normal position. Do this 2–3 times. Good to use at the first signs of tightness or tension in the shoulder and neck area.

To complement the running routine, use the upper-body stretches from the swimming routine.

CREDIT: BOB ANDERSON
ILLUSTRATIONS BY JEAN ANDERSON

Running as a cross-trainer:
Back to a three-day week

Jeff Galloway, author of *Galloway's Book on Running* and founder of the Phidippides running store chain (Phidippides was that stalwart Greek messenger who darted 26 miles or so to Athens to announce victory over the Persians and then, according to legend, dropped dead), suggests a three-day running week for cross-trainers. "Running every other day allows sufficient rest and gives your body all the running stress it will need as a cross-trainer," says Galloway. "Besides, that gives you more time for swimming and cycling."

Galloway urges alternating hard/easy weeks and hard/easy days, with each week consisting of a long run, a speed run (or an easy fartlek session, if you're a noncompetitor), and an easy run.

Before elaborating on Galloway's three-day running plan, however, one important point: You must have a backlog of over-distance work first (after working up to three times your goal race distance per week through 10 percent increases and *maintaining* that stress-base plateau for about the same time it took you to build up to it).

Your long, slow distance plateau is more important than ever in running for the much-enumerated stress reasons. Work by the clock and concentrate on pacing instead of mileage. In fact, if you are a nonrunner who simply wants to finish a triathlon, or if you want to reduce the amount of recovery time tough running requires, skip all speedwork and stick to the low end of your target heart rate throughout your training, or time yourself on broken miles to learn faster pacing. Even experienced runners fall victim to shinsplints with too much intense interval work. Get your high-quality experience in swimming or cycling instead. In any case, a minimum of 3 months at your stress plateau is probably a good idea.

After establishing a solid running history, try Galloway's hard/easy combinations. Here are two of Brad's sample weeks as he prepared for a 10K at the end of his goal triathlon.

Hard week
  1. *Long day.* Monday: 12-mile run.
  2. *Speedwork.* Wednesday: 6–8 sprints (200–440 yards) on a 440–yard track, 5–7 seconds faster than your usual pace.

3. *Fun day.* Friday: a scenic on-and-off fartlek run 5 miles up the coast.

Easy week
1. *Long day.* Monday: 8-mile run.
2. *Speedwork.* Wednesday: substitute a 3-mile run.
3. *Fun day.* Friday: 10K cross-country-type run up the coast.

Notes
1. Speedwork sessions should always be limited to *one* per week.
2. Try to schedule your complete day of rest from all training *after your running long day.*
3. Alternate hard/easy weeks until you're ready to begin your preevent taper. Then cut back to shorter, easier distances again.

The long day
Your week's long run should be up to or beyond the goal distance you are training for. As we saw in the case of Brad's 10K goal at the end of a triathlon, he wants to build up to at least 8 miles on his long day (if you're very experienced and want top results, aim for 15–18). Run 18–22 miles on this day for a half-marathon, or 24 miles for a full marathon (or 28–30 for maximum results).

Watch your weekly long-day totals. Don't let them increase by more than 5 percent from one week to the next, and consider long days only every other week when you just start out.

The speed day
(Optional—use only if your goal is a marked improvement in your running times. This category presents your greatest risk of injury of all speed suggestions in this book. You may wish to substitute a timed middle-distance session instead, or break up a mile or 10K into timed segments and work on keeping a constant pace.)

Before any of the following high-quality run sets, always warm up by jogging very slowly for 10–20 minutes.

Track intervals
Head for your neighborhood's nearest quarter-mile track, and bring along a stopwatch. If you're planning to run 5–13 miles at the end of your triathlon, try the following after your warm-up.

1. Run 4–6 accelerations of 220–330 yards each on the 440-yard track. In each acceleration, gradually increase your speed for

the first 50–80 yards, then hold a fast pace (about the speed you want to hit in the repetitions described in No. 2) for about 70–80 yards, and then slow into an easy jog. Jog as long as you wish between accelerations.

2. Start with 6–8 × 440 yards about 5–7 seconds faster than you want to average in your race. For example, to train for an 8-minute-per-mile pace, run these 440-yard speed repetitions at 1:55. Take as much rest as you wish between each, preferably "active" rest—a walk or slow jog to hasten removal of lactic acid from the muscles.

Notes

1. Cool down slowly after running intervals.

2. Limit these to one per week for a *maximum of 8 weeks in a row.* Then cycle back to long, slow distance work.

3. Remember that interval work should account for no more than 5 percent of your total weekly mileage.

Broken 10K's

Julie Moss suggests running your goal 6.2 miles in thirds. Run each 2-mile segment faster than the previous one, with a 4-minute standing rest in between. "Want to work on transitions?" she says. "Do a 25-mile time trial on your bicycle on your long day, then jump off and run for 30 minutes."

4 × 1's: Run 4 minutes slightly slower than race pace, then do 1 minute full-on sprint.

5 × 3's: Go about 10–15 percent off race pace for 5 minutes, followed by a 3-minute all-out sprint. No recovery jog! This fartlek training simulates what you'll actually be doing in a race.

Reduced-mileage "long days"

If you find you don't have the time for your hard week's long-run day, try to time a reduced-mileage "long day" at a faster clip.

Hill bounding

If this is your first year of cross-training, consider saving this one for next season. Running uphill will force you to perform closer to your anaerobic threshold; for a minimum time investment, your cycling strength and running times will drastically improve. Confine hill work to the off or early season, when you are concerned with quality and strength rather than speed.

Gary Peterson (left) and Scott Molina run hills together at least once a week. Dog Maggie, in background, joins for the first few laps.

STEVE POCIUS

1. Find a gradual slope ¼–½ mile long with an incline of 5–8 percent.

2. Make sure your heels touch the ground as you run up the hill, and try to lift your knees and pump your arms.

3. Try running up the hill three to four times during the first few workouts. It's not going to be easy (try to picture Mariel Hemingway's grace and power when she did hill running in *Personal Best*).

4. Follow hill bounding with lots of stretching and one to two days of recovery afterward.

5. After three or four weeks, try running up and down four to six times, and throw in a shorter and steeper hill for variation from time to time.

6. A month or so before competitive season, concentrate on intervals to improve speed. "By then," says Scott Molina, "thanks to the hill workouts, you will be exhibiting better form in long runs, greater cycling strength in your quadriceps and gluteals, and the physiological and emotional readiness you'll need when you encounter hills in the race itself."

7. Don't bound downhill. It's too hard on your knees. Settle into an easy, heel-first effort.

"My training partner, Gary Petersen, and I don't always look forward to our 'mountain madness' sessions," says Molina. "But then Gary will remind me that the last one to the top of the hill buys the beer, and we'll have a go of it."

The fun run
Enjoy the scenery! Schedule scenic runs or outings. Make this the most enjoyable running of your three-day plan.

Fartlek running
Play follow the leader, explore interesting turns in the road, relish the freedom of this technique. There's no timing structure, so you'll have to discipline yourself to push yourself into the fast-slow pattern. It's a "pour it on when you feel like it" situation. Scott Tinley advises sprinting for lightpoles, stop signs, or cold beers.

"I'll never forget the time a group of us were running and I thought we had lost a friend several miles back," says Tinley. "All of a sudden we were surprised by a giant aluminum trash can rolling down a driveway at us. Practical jokes while running have the distinct advantage of giving people the desire to sprint ahead. After all, you need a head start if you want to emerge from behind a hedge with a hose turned on full blast."

Use the balance and variety of Galloway's cross-training running program to keep your training fun as well as productive. Then test the results by running a pace check on your progress.

1. If your multisport event ends in a 10K and you want to run 6:30 miles, try six 1-milers on the track holding to a 5:20–5:30 pace without going into oxygen debt. (This is extremely fast and is only an example. If you find yourself going too fast into oxygen debt, change your goal times.)

2. On your next long day, time each mile in a nonstop 10K and see if you can keep a continuous 6:30 pace over the 6.2 miles.

3. Gradually cut down your rest time.

4. Test yourself two weeks later to see your improvement.

Books and Periodicals

Running Commentary
   Joe Henderson
   130 East 34th Place
   Eugene, OR 97405
   Newsletter
The Runner
   One Park Avenue
   New York, NY 10016
Running Times
   14416 Jefferson Davis Highway
   Suite 20
   Woodbridge, VA 22191
   (703) 491-2044
Publishes running calendar and occasionally a triathlon calendar
Runner's World
   Box 366
   Mountain View, CA 94042
Good magazine for novice and experienced runners alike
Ernst van Aaken
   Van Aaken Method
   Runner's World, Mountain View, CA 94040, 1976
Manual on endurance running

Runner's Training Guide
    Runner's World, Mountain View, CA 94040, 1973
Guide to basic training
James F. Fixx
    The Complete Book of Running
    Random House, NY, 1977

Organizations

ARRA (Association of Road Racing Athletes)
    1460 Paulsen Bldg.
    Spokane, WA 99201
American Running and Fitness Association
    2420 K St. NW
    Washington, DC 20037
Road Runners Club of America
    1111 Army Navy Drive
    Arlington, VA 22202
The Athletics Congress (TAC)
    155 W. Washington St.
    Suite 200
    Indianapolis, IN 46204
    (317) 638-9155

PART 3

Game Plans

Magicians can do more by means of faith than physicians by the truth.

—Giordano Bruno (1548–1600)

There's no such thing as hitting the wall. All it means is that your mental training has snapped.

—Dave Scott, 30, Davis, CA
Three-time Ironman champion

Schemes, Plots and Flights of Fancy: Keying up for a personal cross-training season

Few beginning triathletes make the mistake of doing too little. Instead, they confuse consistency's slow-but-steady progress with plodding, and opt for headlong overtraining and early burnout—the "fad diet" approach instead of a rational lifetime commitment to cross-training.

Although we clearly understand the concept of a training season and off-season for professional teams, we never stop to apply it to ourselves as average-fitness athletes because we lack that banner event at which to direct our year's training. It leaves our exercising static and uneventful.

The best way to give cross-training vitality is to apply the hard/easy formula not only to weekly schedules, *but to the entire year*. Plan months of easy aerobics followed by intense peak training and then a taper before your goal event, if you have one. It doesn't have to be earthshaking. If you're afraid of open water, your goal could be to swim ¼ mile parallel to shore at the end of your first training season. If you're shy about entering races, it could be to register for your first 10K. Follow Jack Riley's example and devise your own triathlon. Almost anything can serve as your "season-ending meet" to build your confidence and enthusiasm for all ensuing personal seasons.

Emphasize different sports at different times of the year. Just because you're capable of speedwork in swimming, cycling, and running doesn't mean you must always perform at fever pitch. Certainly, no professional athlete can sustain high-stress training all year—why should you? Three sports can also quickly become as boring as one unless you scramble them around at various intensities throughout your year. The groundwork/build/climax/denouement formula for writing a good story (remember the picture of the roller coaster in your grammar-school English textbook?) applies to practically everything that captures our fancy. Aside from the obvious sexual connotation, we've come to expect this same suspenseful delivery in everything from a symphony to a ride on the merry-go-ground. Make a story out of your cross-training to keep yourself your own captive audience.

Periodization of training

Jim Montgomery, coach of the Lone Star Masters swimming team in Dallas, gives a perfect example of how and why fitness athletes should invent this sort of athletic storyline. Montgomery was trying to regroup after his gold-medal-winning 49.99 for the 100-meter freestyle during the 1976 Montreal Olympics, which made him the first person in the world to break the 50-second mark in that event.

"Even during the Olympics, though, I knew a certain period in my life was ending," says Montgomery, now 29. "My days of 4- and 5-hour workouts would soon be over, and I'd have to start earning a living like everyone else. I wanted to find a way of keeping my times as fast as possible, given the limited amount of time I would have for swimming."

He teamed up with LeBaron Caruthers, formerly of Southern Methodist University and now the strength coach for the New England Patriots, to devise a yearlong dry-land work and swimming program. They realized that a proper "mixed bag" would add up to greater results during reduced pool time. Not incidentally, it added a whole new dimension for Montgomery's Masters team (adults 25 and older of all skill levels), who might otherwise have remained blasé about their exercise. Different weeks and months emphasized different types and intensities of training.

This *cycle planning,* also called *periodization of training,* interspersed rigorous periods of high-quality swimming, including some twice-daily workouts, with the reward of slower months of either easy swimming or none at all. The peak swimming months were planned with the twice-yearly Masters National Meets in mind, but most of Montgomery's students were noncompetitors who followed the well-rounded schedule because it gave them the best overall conditioning possible. They would be hard pressed to get that sense of "year-end graduation" from climbing into the pool and doling out the same kind of intervals all year long.

"You can aim for a lake swim, postal event, or even your own timed long-distance session," says Montgomery. "Fit periodization of training to your needs."

The Lone Star Masters could forge through the savage weight lifting in October knowing that they were getting the year's most demanding strength work out of the way. They stretched out their stressed muscles during this opening part of their season through easy distance swimming. After that, they built up to the midseason meet through harder pool intervals while reducing dry-land work. Since building a strong weight-lifting foundation in the fall, they saved time by resorting to fewer weight-lifting days per week, concentrating on fewer repetitions but with heavier weights.

The Nationals, in May and August, determined the peak swimming and tapering weeks. September, after the last big meet of the season, was a complete vacation month, with nothing tougher than water games allowed. Montgomery's cycle planning took the life-beyond-athletics approach by banning all overload efforts around Christmas time. The first half of January was spent back on stroke technique and over-distance swimming to get his postrevelry students back into preholiday shape. Throughout the year the team planned clinics on stroke work or nutrition in addition to social events to make fitness an even more intrinsic part of their lives.

The following diagram shows the intensity match-ups in a typical year with the Lone Stars.

Sizing Up Training Intensity

Putting both the swimming and the strength training cycles together over the year would result in the following graph, which illustrates emphasis *in terms of intensity* in any given month:

TRAINING INTENSITY

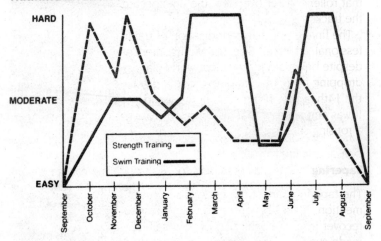

Use Jim Montgomery's cycle planning method to plot a year of cross-training, emphasizing different sports and different intensities at various months.

DESIGN: PATTI BENNER

Add two more sports to the combination for cross-training, and your cycle-planning graph could look like a game plan for three-dimensional chess. Think through a reasonable season for yourself, using Montgomery's model of peaks and valleys and ample holiday breaks. Buy a graph-paper notebook and colored pens and give immediate shape to your plans by sketching them out. If you're not enough of an organizer to take pen to actual paper, at least file a rough yearlong cycle of base/build/peak/taper/goal/vacation in the back of your mind. Obviously, you should never leap from vacation or sporadic exercising straight into intense interval work. Your heart and general cardiovascular health require that you build back up to peak form.

Plan *less* than you think you can manage, not more. Since you're ambitious enough to cross-train in the first place, restraint may come harder than you think. But it's far better for novice triathletes to succeed at their intended goals and feel excited by adding more than to fail at their objectives and need to cut back. Allow for skiing and camping trips and out-of-town guests. Don't neglect the virtues of occasionally sleeping in. If your season has that roller-coaster overview, the unexpected won't throw you off the track.

The final proof that periodization of training works for nonprofessional athletes? Size up Montgomery's goal of staying fast despite being older than most world-class swimmers and despite dropping from 4 hours of exercise a day to 1. In 1981, he swam the 14th fastest 100 meters in the world—as a Masters swimmer. It was ample proof that his curtailed cross-training year had been a rousing success.

Tapering

The tapering part of the cycle is so crucial that it merits special mention. It's a session of complete rest to allow your body to recover from the peak part of your self-designed season. You've made such a taxing demand on your muscles with the toughest swimming, cycling, and running workouts of the year that, holding to the general adaptation principle, your muscles must now repair themselves in order to perform at that peak level or beyond.

Once your body recovers through rest, it starts demanding, like a caged lion pacing and clawing at the door, that you feed it what it has come to expect. Expertly timed tapering should have you chomping at the bit by race day. When you finally unleash yourself, you should be so raring to go that you hardly know where all your energy is coming from.

If you're well prepared for your race or goal-distance trial, it's probably better to err on the side of too much rest. Some of you will do better taking a week or more completely off, whereas some professional triathletes argue that complete rest is too much of a shock to a body accustomed to long daily workouts. They'd rather spin in low gear, swim easy miles, and enjoy running just to keep their bodies in line.

Don't be afraid to experiment, but remember that those who

can't resist working hard until race day, thinking that it will give them a tougher competitive edge, will turn in a mediocre performance. What follows next is not a pretty picture. In the true spirit of a vicious cycle, these athletes figure, in varying degrees of disgust, that if they'd only pushed a little more in training this wouldn't have happened. They go out and rack up mileage like mad, do worse next time out, and finally feel they've no choice but to surrender to the ravages of aging.

The last few days of tapering are traditionally reserved for another misunderstood athletic ritual—carbohydrate loading, or saturating the muscles with glycogen so there's more energy to burn during the race. The reason this works to the point that many athletes now load up on spaghetti instead of steak—so much for yesteryear's he-man theories on nutrition—are discussed in the next chapter.

Sample scheduling

Here's how top triathlete JoAnn Dahlkoetter would plan a year's training for a beginner, followed by a sample training week by Mark Wendley, a veteran of many triathlons and a director of a popular cross-training camp.

Training for Your First Short-Distance Triathlon

The following training schedules suggested by JoAnn Dahlkoetter give specific model workouts for the first week of training; for the middle of phase 1, 2, and 3; and for the prerace tapering.

PHASE 1 (Month 1 & 2)
Week 1 sample workout

	Monday	Tuesday	Wednesday	Thursday	Friday	Saturday	Sunday
Swim (yards)	500		500		500		500
Bike (miles)		5		5		5	
Run (miles)	1		1		1		

Week 1 Distance
Swim 2000 yards
Bike 15 miles
Run 3 miles

No. Workouts/Week, Week 1
Swim 4
Bike 3
Run 3

PHASE 1 (Month 1 & 2)
Midphase sample workout

	Monday	Tuesday	Wednesday	Thursday	Friday	Saturday	Sunday
Swim (yards)	Swim 200 Kick 200 Pull 200 (arms only) Total 600		2 × 500	Swim 400 Kick 200 Total 600		1000 continuous	2 × 400
Bike (miles)	10		12		10		13
Run (miles)		3		3		4	

Midphase Weekly Distance
Swim 4000 yards
Bike 45 miles
Run 10 miles

No. Workouts/Week
Swim 5
Bike 4
Run 3

Phase 1 Weekly Range
Swim 2000–5000 yards
Bike 15–50 miles
Run 3–15 miles

PHASE 2 (Month 3 & 4)
Midphase sample workout

	Monday	Tuesday	Wednesday	Thursday	Friday	Saturday	Sunday
Swim (yards)	Swim 300 Kick 300 Pull 300 Swim 100 Total 1000	2 × 500	5 × 300	1000 continuous	10 × 100		2000 LSD (1.2 mile) in open water
Bike (miles)		20		10		30 LSD in hills	15
Run (miles)	3		5		8		4

Phase 2 Weekly Range
Swim 4000–10,000 yards
Bike 50–100 miles
Run 12–30 miles

Midphase Weekly Distance
Swim 7500 yards
Bike 75 miles
Run 20 miles

No. Workouts/Week
Swim 6
Bike 4
Run 4

PHASE 3 (Month 5 & 6)
Midphase sample workout

	Monday	Tuesday	Wednesday	Thursday	Friday	Saturday	Sunday
Emphasis	Rest day	Bike hard	Run hard	Swim hard	Run long	Bike long	Swim long Transition Training 2500 (1.5 miles) open water
Swim (yards)	2 × 500 easy	Swim 300 Kick 300 Pull 300 Swim 300 Pull 300 Total 1500	5 × 400 each one faster	All swim: Slow 400 Fast 10 × 100 Slow 100 Total 1500	Swim medium (20-sec. rest) 2 × 100 2 × 200 2 × 300 1 × 200 1 × 100 Total 1500		

Bike (miles)	20 easy	50 LSD in hills	25 easy
Run (miles)	5 easy	10 LSD in hills	7 easy

Slow 5
Fast 15
Slow 5

Slow 2 miles
Fast
4 × 440 yards
2 × 880 yards
1 × 2 mile
(60-sec. rest in between)
Slow 2 miles
Total 8 miles

Phase 3 Weekly Range
Swim 8000–12,000 yards
Bike 80–150 miles
Run 25–45 miles

Midphase Weekly Distance
Swim 10,000 yards
Bike 120 miles
Run 30 miles

Prerace taper schedule
One week prior to race: all easy workouts

	Monday	Tuesday	Wednesday	Thursday	Friday	Saturday	Sunday
Swim	1000	1500	2000	1500	1000	Rest	Race!
Bike	20		20		15	Rest	
Run		5		3		Rest	

A Triathletic Training Week

This training program suggested by Mark Wendley of the National Triathlon Training Camp, is a sample training week for a short triathlon. If you pace yourself properly during the event, you'll finish tired—like everyone else—happy, and ready to enter your next triathlon.

Remember, this is only an example of a minimum program designed for busy people. You can add to these workouts or switch them around, as your spare time allows.

Monday	Tuesday	Wednesday	Thursday	Friday	Saturday	Sunday
Up 7:30	Up 6:30 BIKE 11 miles (1 hour)	Up 7:30	Up 6:30 BIKE 11 miles (1 hour)	Up 7:30	Up 7:00 BIKE 10 miles to swim workout and back	Up 7:00 BIKE 35 miles (3 hours)
Work 9–5 RUN 4 miles (40 min.)	Work 9–5 SWIM 3000 yards (1 hour)	Work 9–5 RUN 8 miles (1½ hour)	Work 9–5 SWIM 3000 yards (1 hour)	Work 9–5 RUN 6 miles (1 hour)	SWIM 3000 yards (2 hours total for swim and bike)	

Week's Totals:
Swimming 9000 yards
Biking 67 miles
Running 18 miles
Hours 12 hours, 10 minutes (approximately)

NATIONAL TRIATHLON TRAINING CAMP
1015 Gayley Ave. Suite 217
Los Angeles, CA 90024

INDIVIDUAL TRIATHLON TRAINING PACKET:

Steps for Establishing a Triathlon Training Program:

1. Consult a physician for a physical examination.
2. Establish long-term and short-term goals. Goals should be challenging
   but, most importantly, realistic.
3. Set up a training log (copy attached) and establish your weekly
   training routine (see attached "Triathlon Training Schedule" form).

Goals:

LONG-TERM GOALS: To be achieved by the end of the season, year, etc.

Break 13 hours in the IRONMAN!

Swim: 1:10 / Transition: 10 min / Bike – 7:00 / Transition: 10 min / RUN – 4:25 Total: 12:55

SHORT-TERM GOALS: Steps on the climb to the summit of your long-term goal.
                   (Example: Run a 10K in under 40 minutes, Swim a mile
                   without stopping, etc.)

1. *Break 20 minutes in 1650 yd. Freestyle* Date achieved: 3/9/83 (19:51.93)
2. *Break 3 hours in a U.S.T.S. race.* Date achieved: 6/25/83 (2:55.01) USTS- L.A.
3. *Finish top 20 in ANY RACE.* Date achieved: 10/2/83 (4th)
                                         U.S. Amateur Champs
                                         @ L. Havasu!

Triathlon Log: (copy attached)

Logs are important for guaging your progress during training. Use the
"Comments" column for recording times, how you feel during workout, injuries,
your weight, etc. Be sure to photocopy the form before using it, one page
for each month of the year.

Triathlon Training Schedule: (copy attached)

1. Fill in the pertinent times during the day in the left-hand column.
2. Fill in your time commitments for work, family & friends, and other.
3. Then schedule your workouts. Remember, it is not essential to do
   all three sports every day. Mix up your workouts to give specific
   muscle groups a chance to recover and to keep your routine fresh.
   Most of all, have fun!

Training logs

We're prisoners of a certain report-card mentality, and it isn't such
a bad way to go. We need visible and viable evidence that we're
doing well and the gratification of seeing our progress—if not
recorded for posterity, then at least to cheer ourselves up when
we're feeling generally moody and ineffectual. That's where your
cycle-planning graphs and training diaries come in. If you want a

Conversion:
(meters → yards : ÷ .9144)

TRIATHLON TRAINING LOG
AUGUST , 19 83

NATIONAL TRIATHLON TRAINING CAMP

DATE/DAY	SWIMMING (in yards)	BIKING (in miles)	RUNNING (in miles)	COMMENTS:
8/1/83 Mon.	ø yds	ø mi	ø mi	
2 Tues.	≈3280	11	ø	Bike San Vicente / Swim @ S.M.C. LONG COURSE
3 Wed.	ø	11	4.5	" −RAIN! / Run San V.
4 Thurs.	≈3280	11	ø	
5 Fri.	ø	ø	ø	
6 Sat.	≈2410	ø	4.5	S.P.M. L.C. Regional Swim Championships / 1500 M. FREE 20:38.55
7 Sun.	ø	11	ø	
8 Mon.	ø	11	4.5	
9 Tues.	≈3060	25	ø	Bike in Thousand Oaks Hidden Valley Loop (1:38:20) / Swim @ SMC Good Hill Workout!
10 Wed.	ø	ø	4.5	
11 Thurs.	≈2410	11	ø	
12 Fri.	ø	11	ø	
13 Sat.	≈1970	ø	ø	SPA L.C. Regional Swim Championships @ Irvine / 200 m FREE 3rd 2:22.85 / 400 m FREE 5th 5:07.08 / 200 m BACK 1st 2:45.33
14 Sun.	≈1970	ø	ø	
15 Mon.	ø	ø	4.5	
16 Tues.	≈3060	11	ø	
17 Wed.	ø	11	4.5	San V. Run time: 38:42
18 Thurs.	≈3940	ø	ø	
19 Fri.	ø	ø	4.5	Interval work: fast/slow quarter miles
20 Sat.	3200	11	ø	Swim @ SMC. Short Course
21 Sun.	ø	58	ø	Bike PCH w/ Tom Peters (4:30)
22 Mon.	ø	ø	4.5	
23 Tues.	3100	11	ø	
24 Wed.	ø	11	4.5	Interval work in Run
25 Thurs.	3500	ø	ø	Swim @ SMC. (workout included 8×200's on 2:40)
26 Fri.	ø	11	8.5	Run San V. to Ocean (1:15:43) Good Run No Pain!
27 Sat.	3600	11	ø	
28 Sun.	ø	58	ø	Bike PCH of Judy & Laurie (4:58) Time includes 32 min stop to change rear flat tire. 29 mile split − 1:59.
29 Mon.	ø	11	4.5	
30 Tues.	4000	ø	ø	Swim workout included 1000 Free in 12:30.0
31 Wed.	ø	ø	ø	
MONTH TOTALS:	42780 yds	328 mi	53.5 m (✱)	
WEEKLY AVE.: (4.43 weeks in August)	9657 yds/wk	74.0 mi/wk	12.1 mi/wk	(✱) Running mileage in "rebuilding" phase after injured right achilles tendon in July.

more official-looking training log than a spiral notebook, they only cost a few dollars at most sporting-goods stores. Virtually all top athletes swear by them.

Following one of this book's central choruses, record mileage within the framework of hours—how many miles you managed

TRIATHLON TRAINING

SCHEDULE:

TIME:	MONDAY	TUESDAY	WEDNESDAY	THURSDAY	FRIDAY	SATURDAY	SUNDAY
6:00–7:00 am							
7:00– 8:00		BIKE 11 miles	BIKE 11 miles	BIKE 11 miles	BIKE 11 miles	SWIM @ S.M.C.	
9:00 am–5:00 pm	WORK			WORK			Long BIKE Ride
5:00–6:00 pm.							
6:30 pm.		SWIM @ S.M.C.	RUN san vicente	SWIM @ S.M.C.	RUN san vicente		

within a certain time limit. Write down the terrain you covered. Cycling 20 miles through the hills is bigger guns than 20 miles on a flat highway. What was the weather like? Running 5 miles in 80-degree high-noon weather on pavement isn't exactly 5 miles in a 65-degree sunset breeze under the elms on a soft dirt road. What times of day does your running seem strongest? Is your resting pulse rate dropping? Have dietary changes affected your training? How are you feeling generally? Do you need to reevaluate your goals?

One technical hint: Something in our human chemistry makes us more eager to fill in empty boxes or check things off a list than to resort to essay answers. Plan beforehand how to intertwine your running, swimming, cycling, stretching, or strength training over the weeks and months, write it out, and then fill in the blanks and make changes in your diary as you go along. To do that requires a clear understanding of what your goals are.

Goal setting

All goal setting means in cross-training is deciding what you want to do and the best way of getting there. We're brilliant when it comes to long-term aims, although we could probably stand to be more specific. Thinking, "I want to make a lot more money" is fine, but thinking, "I am going to make $6000 more by next December than I am making this year" is better.

In the first instance, saying, "I want to" is far weaker than saying, "I am going to." And "a lot more money" is vague enough that you don't have to risk failure by ever stating what constitutes your idea of success. Pin floundering aims onto definite numbers and times. Define the pact. If you can't even picture it, how are you supposed to go after it?

Enter in short-term goals, and here's where we become less brilliant. They're no less than the plan of attack, the precise checkpoints you've decided are necessary in order to achieve the larger goal.

Here are some guidelines in pinning them down.

1. Write down all the steps you must undertake to achieve your larger objectives. Literally spelling them out will give definition to your progress. If your long-term goal is to compete in your first ocean swim but you can't swim a stroke, your short-term goals might be: (1) Take swimming lessons. (2) Practice freestyle until you have a feel for the water. (3) Swim 20 minutes without stopping. (4) Build up to swimming a continuous half-hour. (5) Find a swimming companion who can teach you about open water, etc.

2. Put time limits on everything. Change the numbers as you progress, but start by planning to finish those swimming lessons by June 30. Say that you're going to swim those 30 straight minutes by July 31. That way you can schedule open-water practice at the warmest part of the season, in mid-August.

3. Tell other people your goals. Muhammed Ali's assertive, "I am the greatest" is the classic example of turning declarations into deeds. After convincing a worldwide audience, he had ensured his success.

Mind over matter

Once you've devised your season's schedule and established your goals, sharpen your training focus and maximize your exercise yield through mental conditioning. All top triathletes agree that endurance training and long-distance races are as much in your mind as in your body, and the longer or harder the effort, the greater role mental fortitude plays.

Don't dismiss mental conditioning as outlandish or mystical. Professional athletes and coaches who realize that fitness is a holistic blend of good nutrition and physical and mental skills study relaxation and visualization techniques, and great players are instinctive masters of concentration. When Babe Ruth stepped up to bat and pointed to where in the bleachers he intended to hit a home run, he was announcing his positive intentions to a large audience and backing them up with visualization. In a similar way, your mental conditioning as a triathlete got under way when you imagined your schedule and goals—your announcement of intentions. Now you can use other mental strategies for putting them into action.

The following paragraphs describe the most popular methods used by triathletes to develop mental toughness in attaining their goals and seeing themselves through the rough parts of their seasons.

Positive thinking

"Instead of thinking on the bicycle, 'Don't point your toes in,' think, 'Toes out!' " says Julie Leach. "That replaces a negative statement with a positive one. Your brain picks up on the 'don't' in the first instance, and the main thing that registers is that you're doing something wrong or bad."

Don't start by putting limits on yourself in thinking, "I know I'm not as strong (or fast or young) as everyone else, but...." Expand your potential by focusing on what you *can* do.

Relaxation

If someone asks you to name the capital of Rhode Island, you might think hard, strain through your memory banks, and finally come up empty. "Providence" will snap into your brain as if by magic while you're out driving or watering the ferns and have given up on it. The old adage, "Don't try so hard and you'll do fine" works perfectly in exercise, because only through relaxation can you have a comfortable feel for what you're doing.

Breathe deeply, relax the muscles in your face, and practice what Richard Marks calls "inflow." "We're good at energy outflow in triathloning, but we're bad at replacing it," says Marks. "Try massages or some other reward after a hard day of training. Bathe occasionally instead of showering. Meditate. Athletics is the Western form of meditating, anyway.

"When you exercise, use a bilateral approach. Think of using your right leg to help your left on the bike. Swim with bilateral breathing to avoid stressing one shoulder or arm. Learning this kind of meditative balance and symmetry not only prevents injury, it enhances efficiency."

Localized relaxation

Terry Orlick, author of *In Pursuit of Excellence* (Human Kinetics Publishers, 1980), points out that some athletes can relieve butterflies in their stomachs by tensing and then relaxing the abdominal muscles several times. If your legs are shaky, try tensing and then relaxing the thighs. If you get a stitch in your side while running, slow down and use your breathing to iron it out. Your impulse might be to bend over into the cramp, but it's better to stretch it out slowly. Try applying direct pressure by squeezing the ailing part and then letting it go.

Orlick suggests telling yourself before a race that what you're about to do is the most important event of your life. "I know it isn't," he says, "but pretend for the duration of the event that your life is on the line."

Self-hypnosis

"The hypnotist tells a football player that his hand is stuck to the table and he cannot lift it. It is not a question of the football player 'not trying.' He *simply cannot*," says Maxwell Maltz, author of *Psycho-Cybernetics* (Prentice Hall, 1960). The athlete is as strong as ever, but the power of suggestion is enough to cause contrary muscles to contract against their will.

Hypnosis seeks to remove mental blocks or indoctrinations through positive suggestions. That's it. You can induce a hypnotic state as easily by yourself as with someone else. No gyroscopic reeling or swaying watches involved. It's only a matter of relaxing deeply into a meditative state so that you can make discoveries just the way "Providence," the answer to your nagging question, popped into your head when you least expected it while relaxing.

Once you uncover your subconscious obstacles, you can excise them and replace them with a clear mental image of a desired end. These confident thoughts and pictures of your imagination can then more readily become the realities of your daily existence. That football player can just as easily be told that he is going to throw four touchdowns on Sunday, and that's what he'll be able to see himself doing.

You've experienced a hypnotic or trancelike state many times already in your life. It's nothing more than highly focused concentration. When reinforced with positive thinking, it enables those athletes who are less physically gifted or technically skilled to perform sometimes astounding feats.

Body checks and word cues

We all have our own "mantras," or special code words that we repeat over and over when we need an extra push. Swimming coach James E. Counsilman suggests substituting, "I'm getting tired" or "This is starting to hurt," with, "I can feel my arteries unclogging," "This is helping my heart," "I'm losing weight and getting in shape," etc. One swimmer repeats the words *reach* and *confidence* as her mantra to keep her arm pull efficient, since she tends to shorten her reach when tired.

When doing long-endurance work, give yourself quick body scans from time to time while maintaining this inner chant. Begin by focusing on your feet. Make sure they're still part of the confederacy. Work your way up for an entire body check—don't forget to loosen the expression on your face—and inject your preselected code words where necessary to relax tense muscles or to talk yourself through the exhausting parts.

Visualization

When platform divers stand in the tower with their eyes closed, it's because they won't leap until they see themselves performing a perfect dive. The more you practice this type of visualization, the better you'll become at translating mental images into action.

For example, picture yourself training or racing in a triathlon. Run through a mental checklist of all possible stumbling blocks and alternatives so that nothing will catch you unaware. "Think through all aspects of your training or race preparation," says Mark Wendley. "Go through it, see it, see yourself breaking your best time. If you can't see yourself doing it, it's not going to happen."

To test your aptitude for seeing with your mind's eye, try to picture Lincoln's face on a $5 bill. You've certainly seen it many times, but how well can you reproduce it in your thoughts? Now, study the actual portrait for a moment, close your eyes again, and visualize his face. Be as specific on details as possible. Focus on his gaze and hairline, for example.

Open your eyes and check how accurate your corrections were. Close your eyes once more and continue correcting your mental mistakes until the portrait is as sharp in your thoughts as it is on the bill. Finally, your visualization should be so much in control, and so familiar with the way Lincoln looks, that you can afford to close your eyes and move his gaze or hairline around to create a portrait of your own, knowing you can think it back to "normal" in an instant. The obvious lesson is that you can only change what you have in your command.

Audiovisual picturization

Here is a more advanced technique. Why stop with silent movies? Let's say you form a mental image of your rival in an upcoming triathlon. Immediately make that person come alive in your imagination by giving him or her details—gaze and expression and hairline, the way you did with Lincoln's face. Capture it so precisely that you can then imagine variations from that person's usual pose.

Now picture that person speaking. Go beyond simple visualization and add an audio track. Focus on the person's lip movements to hear what he or she is saying. Begin with a tone or phrase you associate with that person, which can then serve as a link to snatches of conversation.

From there, engage the person in a direct conversation. Use both visual and vocal clues to get a clearer understanding of this person's motives, personality, or stance. If all of this sounds slightly odd or fanatic, remember that it's really only a stylized exercise of what we do with people continually. We are always trying to second-guess someone, predict responses, or draw conclusions based on what a person has been known to say or do in other situations.

Pseudoenvironments

Michael Shermer, in his book *Psychling* (Melton Printing, 1982), a volume on mental fitness for cyclists, cites the work of Gordon Smith in creating "pseudoenvironments"—rooms or workshops in which you set up artifacts that reinforce your goals. If you wanted to learn French, for example, Smith might fill a room with French posters and books and pipe in French music.

Shermer suggests that if you are planning a century ride, you could put up signs all over your designated room that say "100 miles" or "I can ride 100 miles." Posters of people who have done it, or any trophies you might have to remind yourself of your other past successes, should be in this room. When Shermer was training for the Great American Bike Race (from California to New York, and now called the Race Across America), he even put up posters of his competition near his indoor bike and in effect raced his opponents every time he trained.

Finally, when assessing your goals and mental training, make all necessary changes to keep your triathloning hobby realistic. Never compare your goals with anyone else's, and leave plenty of time for family, friends, and other interests.

"Plan your training around your relationships, not the other way around," says Bill Leach. He and his wife, Julie, train for triathlons together and agree that in their case it helps both their marriage and their fitness. "If I were doing this alone, I'd be tempted to quit," says Bill. "I think including your family as much as possible in what you're doing can keep you sane."

Life within doors has few pleasanter prospects than a
neatly arranged and well-provisioned breakfast table.
                                —Nathaniel Hawthorne (1804–1864)

Your plan is to fill a 16-ounce water bottle. Combine in a blender:
  one or two sliced bananas
  1 cup Instant Malt-O-Meal or Cream of Wheat
  ½ cup dried dates
  a few vitamin C tablets (1000 mg)
  1 tablespoon protein powder
  some B_{12} vitamins
  a little instant iced tea
  1 tablespoon ERG
  some potassium tablets
  ½ cup Karo syrup (a slower-burning energy source than sugar)
  (recently excised from recipe: Bufferin and No-Doz)

Liquify and drink. I call this "the meal you don't have to unwrap."

                                —Conrad Will, 42, Del Mar, CA
                                  Triathlon promoter

CHAPTER 8

Long-Distance Fueling: Designing diet for endurance

"What?" says one of the scientists in Woody Allen's *Sleeper*. She and her fellow scientist-of-the-future are discussing American dietary habits of the late twentieth century. "No deep fat frying? They thought hot fudge was *bad?*"

Her partner nods. They shrug and shake their heads with pity.

I live too close to the Pritikin Longevity Center to make a case for junk food—they could be on my doorstep faster than I could swallow a handful of caramels—but *Sleeper's* scientists strike the perfect chord: Today's tonic always seems to be yesterday's poison. What athletes were told to eat a mere 10 years ago for endurance now seems as archaic as the sherry-and-hard-biscuit regimen I once saw recommended in the diary of a turn-of-the-century distance runner.

We've all heard about great athletes who are unabashed about eating whatever junk food they crave, and if a lot of it makes cardiologists cringe, well—wanna race? The proof, as they say, is in the pudding.

For most of us the best formula is somewhere between extremes. What you eat does make a difference in your energy level, and it's possible to change your performance capacity and prolong your life and productivity through good nutrition. But you know all that. The hitch holding us back is the same here as it was for exercising—we think in all-or-nothing terms. We figure we are expected either to adhere to Pritikin's rules every living minute or to make no diet modification whatsoever.

Training

Follow the same rules as you did in cross-training. If your body is accustomed to a certain diet (or level of exercise), that's what it craves. *Make changes gradually.* If you want to cut back on fats and proteins but can't bear to give up red meat every night, try substituting lean meat one or two nights a week. See how it affects your health. Then eat what you want—and if certain dietary changes make you feel better, that's exactly what you'll start wanting.

Finally, never try anything new on race day or before a major event. Don't make abrupt changes or lose too much weight too fast. With that in mind, here are some specific guidelines to use during training for more energetic and longer-enduring exercise.

Proteins versus carbohydrates

If muscles are built from protein, went the most recent way of thinking, then the more protein one ate, the bigger the biceps. It's the same sort of conclusion as drawn by primitive tribesmen who think that eating the heart of a slaughtered lion will make them brave. The athletes on high-protein diets had such impressive muscles because of their training, however. Stressing muscles builds muscle mass—not consuming large amounts of protein.

Protein is actually the least efficient energy source, and it's used only when carbohydrates or fats aren't available. The liver converts excess protein into fat and stores it. Other than supplying small amounts of glucose via gluconeogenesis, it plays no role in the increased metabolic turnover rate that stimulates prolonged levels of physical activity.

The traditional American diet provides such an overkill of protein—certainly if it's energy and endurance you're after—that those high-protein supplements are usually superfluous. Worse, most of the food we think of as "high protein"—cheese is a perfect example—is higher in fat than anything else. After a typical meal of a steak marbled with fat, a baked potato with sour cream, and a salad smothered in dressing, you can almost hear your arteries harden.

Our energy fuel comes in much greater measure from complex carbohydrates, such as whole-grain products, legumes, potatoes, fruits, and vegetables, which the body converts into glycogen and stores in the muscles to use during exercise. These glycogen stores—and your body's ability to pace their use—determine how well you perform in aerobic endurance events.

When these energy stores are reduced, you begin to tire and go slower. If you continue exercising, your body starts breaking down its fat stores as an auxiliary service to your dwindling glycogen stores.

That's when the legendary "hitting the wall" occurs. Dave Scott can declare that it only exists in one's mind because he and other top endurance athletes have conditioned themselves to break down fat with impressive facility. The less trained you are, the more querulous your system becomes when asked to turn to its reserves.

The Pritikin Plan is arguably the best model for a high-energy diet. Nathan Pritikin, who has done extensive work with recovering and potential cardiac patients at his Longevity Center in Santa Monica, advocates that your total calorie intake should be about 70–80 percent complex carbohydrates, only 7–12 percent protein, and 7–10 percent fat. That's a shift from our current estimated national average of 40–50 percent fats, 15–20 percent proteins, and 40–50 percent carbohydrates, based on such staples as red meat, oil, salt, and refined flour and sugar.

The Pritikin Plan is not a vegetarian diet—lean meats and poultry are a good source of protein low enough in fat for Pritikin to recommend them. Many top triathletes adhere to his plan. The problem with the Pritikin diet is that it may be the ideal way to stave off a heart attack, but it's so strict that it's impossible not to fall off the wagon occasionally.

Just try to stay within the spirit if not the letter of the law. Even the U.S. Senate, in its recently released U.S. Dietary Guidelines, recommended that Americans increase their complex carbohydrate consumption to at least 55–60 percent of total caloric intake, and cut back on fats and salt by 50–85 percent. (The more processing involved in a food, the higher the sodium content, which is used for flavor and preserving. Pickles, cheeses, and canned and frozen foods have more sodium in one serving than your body needs for days on end.)

In summary: Fuel for endurance exercise comes chiefly from complex carbohydrates. Whole grains, legumes, potatoes, fruits, and vegetables should constitute well over half of your diet. Restrict your protein intake to lean meats, fish, and nonfat milk products as much as possible. Drastically reduce your fat intake, and you'll find your energy level increases tremendously.

Your metabolic transport system is responsible for moving glycogen throughout your body through the bloodstream to the muscles that need it at the time. The more highly conditioned your metabolic system, the better it is at rerouting energy to the systems that need it.

Sugar

Glycogen serves as fuel, but your liver must also break some of it down into glucose to keep your blood-sugar level constant, because your brain requires a constant supply. Your muscles may be able to rely on fat during extended exercise, but at that point you must still have some kind of carbohydrate in your bloodstream to feed your brain.

Your liver normally retrieves glycogen from the blood; it can't extract it directly from the muscles. When not enough is being released by the muscles to be of any use to the liver, your central nervous system issues a warning in the guise of dizziness, nausea, or a sensation that you're about to black out—hypoglycemia. This usually is only a threat when exercise time exceeds 3 hours.

Sugared drinks are one way to avoid hypoglycemia if you've been exercising for such an extended time. You need water both to dilute the sugar and for fluid replacement. Ellen Coleman, program director of the Riverside Cardiac Fitness Center and the author of *Eating for Endurance* (Rubidoux Printing, 1980), recommends that the more sugar in the drink, the more water you'll need to facilitate absorption. Dilute sugar solutions can be absorbed almost as quickly as plain water, but high concentrations of sugar should be washed down with lots of water.

That's because your body cannot absorb more than about 50 grams of sugar in 1 hour (200 calories). A homemade solution should not contain more than 3 rounded tablespoons (50 grams) in each hour's supply. Coleman, who has devised the nutritional schemes of countless top athletes training for endurance events, advises that this means the drink should not contain more than 2.5 percent sugar, and should be taken *early in the event* (*the first hour*), not later when liver glycogen depletion has a chance to get under way.

Experiment with different concentrations during training, but never on the day of a race. Ingesting a small amount of the replacement solution at frequent intervals, every 15–20 minutes, will help avoid gastrointestinal upsets.

Consuming modest amounts of sugar during training won't be a problem but omit sugar entirely from your preevent meal. (The amount of sugar in a glass of juice or ERG isn't enough to cause any problem.) Even a small amount (300 calories), when taken 30 minutes prior to exercise, can cause faster glycogen depletion. That's because your body responds to the sugar by secreting insulin, which interferes with your ability to use your body fat for energy. You are therefore forced to rely more on muscle glycogen and will burn it up faster.

Sugar ingestion during exercise, however, won't interfere with your body's use of fat nor will it increase your rate of glycogen depletion, because once you start exercising, you suppress the release of insulin.

In *summary*: In exercise over 3 hours, avoid hypoglycemia by ingesting sugared drinks (no more than 50 grams—about 3 tablespoons—of sugar per hour). Avoid sugar in a preevent meal, because it stimulates the production of insulin, which interferes with the body's ability to burn fat. You can ingest sugar during long-duration exercise because the exercise suppresses the release of insulin. As we'll see later, water, not sugar, is your chief nutritional concern in shorter events.

Vitamins and minerals for endurance

The argument as to whether or not you should take vitamin supplements to improve athletic performance continues. Your needs are probably adequately met by a well-balanced diet, and unless a deficiency already exists, supplements are unnecessary. Others swear by them, arguing that our soil is so depleted of minerals that they're essential for optimum fitness.

Taking supplements is strictly a matter of choice. Remember that overloading all at once on water-soluble vitamins (such as B and C) will just give you expensive urine, and extreme overdoses of fat-soluble vitamins that are stored in the body (A, D, E, K) can be toxic. Mineral supplements should be taken only under a doctor's supervision, as our bodies require only trace amounts. Too much will do you more harm than good.

Ergogenic supplements: The so-called superathlete foods or diet boosters, such as wheat-germ oil, bee pollen, or vitamin E derivatives, might make positive contributions to your diet, but they aren't going to make up for inadequate training or unsound nutrition.

B-complex vitamins: Endurance training increases the need for B-complex vitamins. Whether or not you choose to take a supplement, eat foods rich in vitamin B.

B_1 (thiamine): cereal grains, wheat germ, pasta.
B_2 (riboflavin): yeast, milk, liver, dried peas and beans, fruit, leafy vegetables.
B_3 (niacin): poultry, tuna, nuts, eggs.
B_6: spinach, green beans, bananas, fish, potatoes.
B_{12}: animal foods and nutritional yeast.

Iron: Athletes sweat away a substantial amount of iron during prolonged activity. Women in particular might wish to ask their doctor about using an iron supplement and regularly consume high-iron foods such as legumes, dried fruits, whole grains, green leafy vegetables (raw spinach is excellent), and lean meats.

Potassium: Endurance exercise will also make you sweat away potassium, magnesium, and calcium. Replace them, especially during heavy training or hot weather, by bolstering your diet with more potassium-rich foods, such as citrus fruits, bananas, and potatoes.

It's the cumulative effect of losing these minerals that matters. Several days of hard training or a very long-endurance event will sweat them out of you, but you don't need to worry about adverse effects or replacement needs during events under 3 hours or in regular training. A normal diet will replace sodium lost during average exercise. If you cramp during a short race, it's probably because of dehydration, not a potassium deficiency.

Athletes who drink undiluted electrolytes high in potassium and sodium or who eat salt tablets are only increasing the amount of stress on their cardiovascular systems and kidneys. "The more concentrated the sodium you put into your body during exercise, the more water is pulled toward your digestion and away from your working muscles," says Dr. R. James Barnard, a kinesiologist at the University of California, Los Angeles, who has designed diet plans for long-distance triathletes. "When water is drawn into the stomach during exercise, it can cause nausea." (Note that this nausea results from sodium, and is not a result of drinking plain water during exercise.)

In *summary*: The best route with vitamins and minerals is to maintain a balanced diet; thereafter using supplements is up to you. Emphasize foods rich in B-complex vitamins. Try foods rich in iron and potassium to replace minerals lost through sweat, but don't overload your system with concentrated electrolytes during a short race. Finally, on days before and after heavy workouts, eat at least 70 percent carbohydrates, which should provide you with the necessary nutrients to train with less fatigue.

The caffeine controversy

The ballots haven't all been counted on the caffeine question, either, but David Costill and many others have suggested that a moderate amount (two cups) of coffee prior to a race could possibly aid endurance (but avoid sugar right before your event), since the caffeine inhibits the actions of the enzymes that burn carbohydrates. It may also help break down fats in the blood, thereby delaying glycogen-depletion fatigue.

Coffee can increase muscle tremor, act as a diuretic, and exacerbate your already tense prerace nerves, however. Those opposed to caffeine under any circumstances would as soon drink coffee before a race as fly to Mars, but if you are a guiltfree drinker, experiment with it *during training only* and see how it affects your performance.

It's the water—and not a lot more

The edicts of the President's Council on Physical Fitness ended my high school's desultory softball and pitched us, with confused reluctance, into the abyss of track and field. Miss Baker, our gym teacher, tried in earnest to bring us up to standard, but we were gleefully nonchalant about following her orders. A side bonus was that this drove Miss Baker, responsible for molding the school's entire female population into the image of health mandated by the leader of the free world, to the breaking point.

One morning she wildly shooed us away from the drinking fountain after we'd gamboled a few times around the track. "I've had it!" she thundered. "Anyone dumb enough to drink during track deserves what she gets!"

Even those with a more able-bodied adolescence probably recall a similar warning. According to the general folklore still prevailing during the early 1970s outside athletic circles, drinking water during exercise would provoke stomach cramps and nausea, a health concept that now seems as Victorian as leeching.

Our baser instincts during track turned out to be right on the money, and therein lies the lesson. Listen to your body and you'll probably be right. We now realize that not only is hydration essential during training or racing, it's indispensable at frequent, regular intervals, not merely when you feel thirsty. Studies reveal that losing only 3 percent of your body weight during exercise results in a 50 percent reduction in athletic performance. Water loss approaching 10 percent of body weight is life-threatening.

For long-distance efforts, particularly in hot weather, try hyperhydration. Drink about 1 quart of water about an hour prior to performing, and 8–16 ounces a half-hour or less before your competition or long training session. Replace 200–300 milliliters of fluid at least every 15 minutes during the event. (Carry two water bottles on your bicycle.) Slightly chilled water will be absorbed faster than lukewarm water.

Stick to plain water. Constant fluid replacement, whether or not you think you need it, is your main concern during exercise, not calories. The longer the event, the more you might want to add some sugar diluted according to Coleman's specifications. You can also dilute orange juice or colas with three parts water, or add equal parts water to prepared electrolyte-replacement drinks or vegetable juices.

In summary: Drink water at frequent, regular intervals in *any* race or training session. Don't wait until you feel thirsty.

Race day

Carbohydrate loading

In the strictest sense, carbohydrate loading is preparation for intense activity that will take 3 hours or longer. The underlying principle is to saturate the muscles with as much glycogen as possible—"double-loading" the muscles with extra energy sources.

Athletes used to deplete their muscles of all glycogen stores through peak training at the end of their season. They would then switch to a high-protein diet at the beginning of their taper to increase the manufacture of the enzyme that produces and stores glycogen. Three days prior to the event, they would consume 75 percent carbohydrates in order to ram-feed the muscles with extra energy stores. This type of glut-feeding can be highly stressful, causing fatigue and nausea, and is no longer recommended.

For most athletes, it's enough to rest a few days before the event and maintain a diet consistently high in complex carbohydrates. Don't overeat the night before, or you'll end up sluggish, and avoid spicy foods or fats (including dressings, butter, whole milk, and cheese). Rely on high-carbohydrate foods that you are familiar with and enjoy.

The preevent meal

Eat a small, bland meal of about 500 calories up to 4–5 hours before your competition. At this point your preevent food won't contribute anything to your muscle glycogen and fat stores, so don't try to make up for missing a carbo-load party the night before.

Don't surprise your stomach on race morning. Find out what suits you in training, and stick to that. Oatmeal or some other such flummery is fine because it won't distend your stomach, which can restrict your breathing during exercise, and it won't stay in your digestive tract. Avoid heavy grains, milk products, or butter on race day; they are too hard to digest and will nauseate you even as they sit in your stomach like lead. And remember that sugar taken right before racing can hamper your performance. You need to be exercising before your system can use it properly.

Eating during a triathlon

During races or training sessions between 2 and 4 hours, water is your main concern. Diluted fruit juice can help maintain your glucose level. Eat as sparingly as possible, if at all, and restrict yourself to easily digestible foods.

Fruits or other carbohydrates to boost your blood-sugar level are fine for much longer events. Do virtually all of your eating on the bike (you want to avoid eating on the run) at regular intervals, every 15–30 minutes. Don't wait until you start to feel run down. Fuel yourself as you cycle along with small amounts of food that are appealing enough to encourage you to eat—bananas and cookies or blended fruit drinks are popular favorites. Steer clear of fats. They serve guava jelly sandwiches at the Ironman for a sort of Hawaiian tropical fruit-and-grain repast, but leave the fat-rich peanut butter sandwiches at home. Avocados are probably a mistake too, although some athletes thrive on them even during races.

One hint: When hydrating during your first race, stop, drink the water, and then begin running again (or if you're cycling, make sure that stopping won't impede other competitors). Until you get the hang of it, you're likely to get most of the water on your face as you drink on the run, not in your system.

The postevent meal

Eating after a triathlon is like going off a fast. If it's big enough to take a lot out of you, don't sit down to a large meal right away. You have plenty of time to make up for all those calories you lost. Drink as much water as you can along with some diluted fruit juice after your competition, and give your appetite time to adjust. Then, when your appetite returns, eat a well-balanced meal consisting mainly of complex carbohydrates.

After a race or tough training session, lie down and put your legs up with knees bent. A good many triathletes do it to relax after a long-endurance effort, to redirect the blood's circulation after running, and especially to relieve the tension in the small of the back heightened by cycling and accentuated by running. Besides, if you've come this far you deserve some respite.

A few strong instincts, and a few plain rules.
                              —William Wordsworth (1770–1850)

Race directing is like juggling. The problem is getting everything up into the air in order. After that, it's light. You only have to worry about adjustments—and some luck.

Take our first United States Triathlon Series race three years ago in San Diego. We ordered some orange swim caps from Canada. For some reason they got detoured to Los Angeles, and UPS couldn't find them. Finally, about 9 hours before the race was due to start, they turned up. Cathy Hoy (series public-relations manager) talked the dispatcher into driving them down from L.A. with his girl friend. We got 3 cartons of caps about 6 hours before the gun went off. After that, we realized that the key to success in this business was an indomitable will to overcome . . . and quick feet.

                              —Jim Curl, Davis, CA, 35
                               Bud Light U.S. Triathlon Series
                               race director

CHAPTER 9

A Day at the Races: A newcomer's guide to entering a multisport event

"Okay, Lane 4," yelled the starter. The swim meet was dragging on into its third hour, and hapless No. 4 had jumped the gun. "If I miss 'Hill Street Blues,' it's all your fault!" The timers, fidgeting by this time anyway, eyed the miscreant with exasperation as he pulled himself back up onto the block.

As swim meets go, this one was a breeze. An informal collision between two crosstown Masters teams is about as low-pressure a swimming contest as you can get, but No. 4 had the misfortune of enacting every novice racer's nightmare—a flub derided by all assembled. Who needs it? No wonder most of us consider races about as much fun as a piano recital.

But novice cross-trainers are in luck, because triathlons have circumvented an emphasis on winning from the outset. Of course, the frontrunners operate on a different set of standards, but for most participants simply finishing is a point of pride. Men and women of all ages and skill levels compete together, as in a marathon or 10K. Instead of feeling vulnerable, with all eyes on you as you stand on a swimming block or sprint down a track, there's strength in numbers, a suitable melding of anonymity and independent action.

The start of the United States Triathlon Series race in Portland.

The United States Triathlon Series in particular has made notable strides in encouraging cross-trainers to enter their first triathlons by offering awards to all age-group winners. At every triathlon award ceremony or banquet I've attended, the 40–70 age-group winners are applauded as enthusiastically as the over-all winner. At the 1983 Ironman awards, for instance, the 60–65-group woman was given as sincere a standing ovation as the top 10.

As cross-training grows in popularity, an exponential number of races and race series are being designed to suit novices.

BOB ELLIS

Triathlons are often connected with sports festivals or community drives and fund raisers and are set in a wider and more beautiful range of scenery than virtually all other mass-participation sports. Triathlons are also the most dramatic means of validating your cross-training. If you're new to the game, here are some answers to questions you might have.

Where can I find a suitable triathlon?
If you aren't associated with any sports clubs or associations in your area, now's the time to join. Word travels fast when you're around people with a common interest. There's also a comprehensive calendar of events in *Triathlon* magazine, and single-sport

publications with general listings are beginning to include information on triathlons. If you live in or near a major city, the U.S. Triathlon Series will probably visit your area during the year. Some triathletes in small towns plan vacations around a race and work it into their travel.

Why compete? I'm only in it for fitness.

You may discover something in a race situation you'll never find if you keep it all to yourself. The old "roar of the crowd" can be downright inspiring—there's some Walter Mitty in all of us—and if you bring your family along, it's a way of sharing what you've been doing fitnesswise during the year. Training can get lonely, and showing your support team what you've been up to has a way of validating it all. Besides, it's a good way to close the cycle of your personal season.

Remember that triathlons are races, not survival tests. If you feel utterly destroyed as you cross the finish line, you need either more training or shorter distances. Pick a "tiny tri" you can easily master your first time out and build from there.

Any suggestions for a bad case of butterflies?

Even experienced triathletes get nervous before a race. Sometimes that starts the adrenaline flowing in a way that motivates you, but other times you might feel as if you should curl up in a corner and wait until it's over. Try the following to bolster your confidence.

1. Do as much preparation as possible before race day. You should have received all pertinent information in the mail. In some triathlons it's possible to register by mail or the night before at the race site.

2. Assemble all equipment the night before—bike, swimsuit, goggles, fluorescent swim cap, helmet, cycling shoes, running shoes, running shorts and shirt, food (if necessary), etc. Check over your equipment, particularly your bicycle. Make sure everything is ready to go. Pin your race numbers on your clothes the night before, and don't forget some celebration funds.

3. It seems obvious, but you'd be surprised how many triathletes get flats during a race and don't know how to change tires. Make sure you have practiced changing to a spare long before this.

4. Get to the race site at least 2 hours before the gun. If you need to register on the day of the triathlon, arrive a long time beforehand. Lines build up at entranceways and for restrooms. After registering, come back and set up your equipment. Give yourself time to stretch, drink water, relax, and talk to your friends. Go look over the starting line. If you're new to racing, this relaxing time is crucial.

Will I be insured during the race?
Find out beforehand, but in most cases athletes are not covered by insurance. If you belong to Tri-Fed/USA, one of the sport's governing bodies, you will be covered if the race has been sanctioned by the group. You are not covered during training.

Who will watch my equipment?
The general rule is that you are responsible for your own things. Different triathlons make different stipulations regarding support groups. In some cases, people with tags identifying themselves as your group can get into the equipment area. Mostly, though, race directors are adamant that competitors receive no outside help and that transition areas be kept clear. Check your bicycle and set it up in its proper starting gear before the race. Although organizers can't be responsible for watching everyone's equipment, you won't need to worry too much.

What about bringing food?
If race rules permit it and it's a long race, bag food that you want to eat during the cycling segment. If it's a short race, bring something along for after the triathlon—water, juice, fruit, sandwiches, and cookies are good selections. You won't need it for a race under 2–3 hours, but you may be hungry afterward.

All that clothes changing and transition work sounds confusing.
As Scott Tinley said earlier, it's only a matter of having all your knickknacks collected and laid out ready to go. The shorter the race, the more "streamlined" your outfitting can be. Many triathletes run a short race only in bathing suits, changing from cycling shoes to running shoes for the last segment. Others prefer throwing on a pair of running shorts before they begin cycling. If you're a new triathlete, feeling comfortable and having all your clothing within easy reach is your main concern, not speeding in

and out of the transition area. Slow down, check to see how you're feeling, and get ready for the next leg of the trip.

Dress for the climate. If it's cold, layer your clothing and stick to wool. Don't forget cycling tights to keep your knees warm. Cover your head as well, since you lose a great deal of body heat through your head. In warm weather, wear light-colored, light-weight materials. You might want sunglasses in either case to reduce glare. A hat or visor is a good idea, and be liberal with suntan lotion.

Speaking of the cold, what's hypothermia, and how can I prevent it? Should I gain weight before I try cold-water swimming?

Hypothermia means that the body's core temperature, or the heat surrounding your vital organs, has dropped drastically enough to endanger the function of your heart and brain. Muscle activity through exercise can greatly increase your core temperature, which also explains why we shiver when we become cold. It's an involuntary muscular reaction to heat up the body.

Normally, exercise in cold weather under dry conditions promotes heat production, and the blood vessels in your arms and legs will constrict to conserve heat for the body cavity. Dressing warmly, with many layers to trap air as insulation, offers enough protection. But swimming in cold water can cause the body's temperature to fall rapidly because you're shunting blood furiously into your arms and legs. Shivering in water causes further heat dissipation.

Even if the water's very cold, you can maintain a normal temperature for at least 15 minutes. After that, your blood stops releasing oxygen to the exercising muscles, and your heart rate complicates matters by decreasing. The muscle tissues go into anaerobic metabolism, and the lactic acid buildup precedes cramping and exhaustion. If there is poor circulation to the heart, hypothermia becomes life-threatening.

Watch for these signs: During the early phases of hypothermia, muscle spasms may set in, particularly in your hands and wrists. As you flail around and your stroke becomes less efficient, you're prolonging your exposure. Shivering starts as your core temperature continues to drop. As a feeling of relaxation envelops you, the shivering stops. *That's probably an indication of danger.* It may indicate that your temperature has dropped to 90°F, whether or not you continue to shiver. If you're feeling vague, incoherent, or uncertain where you are, signal for help at once.

Lurching around, confusion, or slurred speech after the swim may indicate a severe condition. Hypothermia victims should be kept as still as possible to avoid setting off a heart arrhythmia. Use thermal blankets or sleeping bags to begin warming the victim while waiting for the doctor.

Gaining weight may be a minimal help, but acclimating yourself to cold water is more than just packing on insulation. Experienced open-water swimmers have developed their thermoregulatory systems to high-grade levels. That's the only true safeguard, although wetsuits are now permissible in some races.

If you don't have much experience with cold-water swimming, put common sense to the rescue.

1. Avoid competitions in cold water (60°F or less) or stick to triathlons with pool swims.

2. If you're in a triathlon involving an ocean swim but you don't live nearby, add more lake swimming to your training.

3. Some triathletes have been known to sit in a bathtub full of ice cubes. This probably exerts a greater psychological effect than anything else. Since you're not swimming in the bathtub, your body merely shuts down normal blood delivery to your inactive arms and legs. It's not the same as actually swimming in the cold.

4. Get to the race site a week before, if possible, to practice ocean swimming with someone more experienced than you. Remember to swim only in areas designated as safe, and never swim alone.

5. Be alert, but don't use fear of hypothermia as a reason to forego a well-staged race in suitable temperatures. Tens of thousands of people enjoy ocean swimming every year with no ill effects whatsoever.

What about the reverse problem—heatstroke?
Hyperthermia is the summer endurance athlete's greatest danger. Some degree of heat fatigue will hit during a race on a hot day, but weakness and fatigue should be reversible when treated with fluid replacement and rest. If you move beyond that and develop dizziness, extreme weakness, gooseflesh, chills, hyperventilation,

cramping, and an unsteady gait, you're in danger of heatstroke. Learning to identify this type of heat stress can mean the difference between life and death.

Be aware that although the classic heatstroke victim shows no visible signs of sweating, well-conditioned athletes may continue to sweat even while in the throes of an extreme case. A victim of heat exhaustion requires immediate medical attention. Don't waste time administering treatment before calling for emergency help, but while waiting for the paramedics, move the athlete to a cool location. Vigorously fan and sprinkle water over his or her body. If the victim is conscious, administer cool (not cold) water. If the victim is unconscious and doesn't appear to be breathing, administer cardiopulmonary resuscitation at once.

Guard against heat exhaustion by hyperhydration before a race, and drink water at frequent, regular intervals. Remember that you've sweated away a lot during the swim without feeling it, and begin fluid replacement at once. If you drink an electrolyte solution during a longer race, dilute it with water. If you don't, dehydration will set in faster as the stomach draws in water to aid digestion. Avoid *any* fluid replacement you haven't already tried in training.

Pace yourself. Modify the intensity of your efforts according to the air temperature and humidity. If your triathlon takes place in a warm climate, you should spend several months in direct preparation. Gradually increase your training time to simulate hot-weather race conditions, or work up over several months to exercising during the hottest time of the day.

Wear well-ventilated clothing. Seventy percent of the cooling effects of your body's sweat evaporation can be lost through improper clothing. Fishnet jerseys or tank tops are fine. Wet clothing actually impedes cooling, so change into dry shirts or shorts as needed.

What about "pushing through the pain"? Where do I draw the line between giving it my all and endangering myself?
Hypothermia and hyperthermia are serious and happen just often enough that you should know as much as possible about them. But if you're adequately trained and in a short race held in moderate temperature conditions, it's extremely unlikely that you'll run into any kind of trouble.

Knowing when to draw the line can be a double-edged sword, however. You're in a triathlon because you want to push yourself beyond your limits. If it's too much of a snap, you won't feel that you've accomplished anything. On the other hand, learn to distinguish between goading yourself along and real injury. No one is going to respect you for ignoring a serious problem to the point that you put yourself out of training for several months. One triathlete puts it best: "The old saying was, 'No pain, no gain.' We've got a new view now—'No brain, no pain.' "

Finish the race if you are not running the risk of injury. Walk in if you need to, even if the cutoff time has come and gone. The sense of completion will eliminate the stream of "if onlys" that would otherwise plague you the next day.

What are some other ways to guard against injury?

Although cross-training can deter and even prevent injury, you still risk overuse or stress problems. Allowing adequate rest and making sure that your running shoes and bicycle fit properly are the best ways of staying out of trouble. If you're vulnerable to blisters, cover them with salve and tape. If they keep recurring in the same spot, toughen your skin with a tincture of benzoin and lubricate it with petroleum jelly. Alternate running shoes during the week, and keep your nails clipped to avoid blackened toenails. Also, don't run through puddles of water to "cool off" your feet. The water will weigh you down instead.

Those mass starts into the water look great from shore, but I'm afraid of getting completely thrashed. I don't want to wait until everyone's out of the way, either. What should I do?

To paraphrase an old saying, if you play with cats, expect to get scratched. Triathlon starts are self-seeded—meaning that it's mucho macho up on the front line. The contenders want the most direct line from where they are to the finish line, and when the gun goes off you'll feel as if you're caught in a human washing machine. Marianne Brems offers these guidelines for dealing with a mass start.

1. Don't panic. Realize that this isn't a sprint, and you'll have enough time to make up later. The greatest cause of panic is the inability to find free swimming space, so position yourself far back or off to the side. You don't have to wait until everyone is

paddling off to the horizon before you join in, though. The crowd will thin out fairly rapidly, and you'll soon have plenty of space.

2. Water cushions blows. Being kicked by another swimmer may cause momentary loss of concentration, but it won't be painful enough to incapacitate you.

3. Don't waste energy readjusting goggles that are knocked askew. Leave them alone or pull them around your neck until you are in open space and can roll onto your back and kick as you readjust them.

4. If you're an experienced swimmer, push up to an anaerobic start for the first 3–5 minutes. Then settle back into an aerobic level. If your pace slows later, at least you've saved time and energy at the beginning.

5. Other swimmers don't get in your way on purpose. Don't waste energy or ruin your first triathlon by getting angry. Running into you slows them down as much as it does you. Calm yourself by breathing deeply and evenly, and settle into your swimming.

6. Go to the water's edge and splash water on yourself before the race. If possible, take a short warm-up swim. You don't want to be surprised by the water temperature when the race starts; this might set a tone of panic that could endure throughout the triathlon.

Should I run through the course the day before?
If you mean swimming, cycling, and running the entire race to see if you can do it, the answer is an emphatic no! *Rest*. If you've trained adequately and feel strong, there's no need to run yourself down when you should be tapering.

But by all means look over the course a day or two before your race. Check out the landmarks that can serve as visual cues in all three segments. If you know there's an apple orchard halfway through the running leg, it might help spur you toward the finish as you near the point of exhaustion. Being aware of your surroundings will give you a better fix on what you're doing. The more you know, the better. Review the map of the course and drive it, if possible. Know the number of roads and the temperature of the water. If you're new in town, make yourself secure there by arriving early enough to know everything from where to get your car fixed to whom you should contact in case of an emergency.

If a drastic climate change is involved, get there at least four days early. If the water is going to be colder than you're accustomed to, wear two caps or the thermal headgear used by surfers or skin divers, if race rules allow it. If you're not used to ocean swimming, find a knowledgeable coach to teach you how to dive under waves. Don't try to leap over them or hope they'll show mercy by going around you. When you "dolphin" under the waves, hold onto the sand if necessary to maintain your position. Then you can come up swimming.

What about warming up and cooling down for a race?
Warm up by light exercising. Then, when your muscles are warmed up, you'll find prerace stretching can control nervousness. Pay particular attention to the areas you know have a tendency to cramp up.

Pre-Triathlon Stretches

1. Calf stretch

2. Achilles tendon stretch

3. Hamstring stretch

BOB ANDERSON

4. Stretch for ankles, hips, Achilles tendon, and lower back

5. Inner thigh stretch

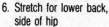

6. Stretch for lower back, side of hip

7. Quadriceps stretch

8. Stretch for quadriceps and front of hip

9. Hamstrings and hip stretch

11. Groin stretch

12. Neck and shoulder stretch

10. Full body stretch

13. Hamstring stretch

14. Hip and lower back stretch

15. Stretch for arms and shoulders

16. Stretch for arm and side

17. Stretch for arms and shoulders

18. Shoulder shrug

After the race, walk some of the lactic acid out of your legs. You'll reduce your recovery rate tremendously by easing out of it instead of succumbing to the temptation of falling over in a heap.

What about handicapped triathletes?

The Bachman Center for the Handicapped in Dallas sponsors an annual triathlon, and the U.S. Triathlon Series has had many handicapped participants. The more organized and established the triathlon, the more likely you are to be accommodated. Check with the race director beforehand if you need special considerations.

If a problem arises during the race, how can I contact the director?

The race director is attending to a hundred small details, and while everyone appreciates a quick salutation of praise or pat on the back, save any constructive comments or criticisms for a letter the next day. There are plenty of volunteers around who can help you deal with any problems that arise.

Even the short distances you've mentioned throughout the book seem like too much. Aren't there any races for people like me?

Yes. Triathloning is a sport that's been growing from the top downward. That takes time, and cross-training is still a relatively new exercise concept. But triple-event races of increasingly smaller dimensions are blooming all over the place. Many groups, for example, are currently devising sprints with maximum distances of ½-mile swim, 12-mile bike, 10K (just over 6 miles) run, and many cities now offer pool swims for those who wish to avoid open water.

Triathlon clubs are excellent sources of "tiny tris." The Nor-Cal club in California recently conducted a 400-meter staggered-start pool swim followed by a 5-mile bike and 1.5-mile run. Word of mouth is your best bet for finding these "10Ks" of triathloning. As cross-training for total body fitness grows in popularity, you'll see a wide array of races to suit everyone.

How hard is it to organize my own triathlon?

Read Sally Edward's and Jim Curl's How to Organize a Triathlon (available for $10.00 postpaid through the Triathlete's Sportshop,

P.O. Box 5338, Santa Monica, CA 90405), and keep in mind that triathlons have so much "festival" atmosphere that they are excellent fund raisers or set pieces for community drives.

If I'm traveling to a triathlon, how can I bring along my bicycle?
When you make an airline reservation, mention that you wish to check a bicycle. This gives the carrier time to allow for extra space in the cargo area. It will cost you $16–$20, which is still cheaper than freight charges. Procedures change, so ask the airline how you should pack your bicycle. Some airlines will supply you with a cardboard container for this purpose, and various lightweight carriers are now being manufactured to suit the needs of roving triathletes. Be sure to check in early, because your bicycle will require extra handling.

It still sounds like a lot of trouble. Quite honestly, I'm afraid of how I'll end up looking.
This sounds suspiciously like a question once put to Doc Counsilman. A swimmer said that he was so mortified at not being able to make flip turns that he fled through the back door when he saw how smooth the swimmers in faster heats had been. Was he being silly? he wanted to know.

I supposed he wanted Dr. Counsilman to say something along the lines of, "No, no, things take time, blah blah blah." But one of this famous coach's most endearing qualities is a certain quiet frankness. "Of course you're being silly," he said. To paraphrase: "Who cares what anyone else thinks? Do you care about anyone low-minded enough to judge your worth as a person on whether or not you can do flip turns? By the way, I've never done flip turns in competition, and I'd better not catch anyone laughing at me."

If all you need is some confidence, try one of these three approaches.

1. Join a triathlon relay team. Some official races allow three-person teams, and you can glide through your best event, get a feel for the atmosphere, and not have to worry about the whole enchilada. It'll give you a prime overview of what happens in a triathlon.

2. Work in tandem with a friend. Have an agreement that the two of you will stick together no matter what. Spell out your

agreement beforehand, and be ready to slow down and wait if your friend falls behind.

3. Be a volunteer at a triathlon in your area. Some of the most fun I've had at a triathlon has been standing behind the tables with various local companies who sometimes compete for prize money awarded the most imaginative or enthusiastic group. The beer flows, they work hard, and in the end most of them decide that it looks so inspiring they're ready to start training. Although the statistics aren't compiled yet on how they feel about it the next day, it may be all you need to take the edge off your apprehensions.

"Let me tell you something, sweetheart," a woman once said to me as she and her fellow bank tellers busily handed off cups of water at a Yosemite triathlon, "I've never seen so many gorgeous men in all my born days." Haven't I said all along that the scenery is one of cross-training's great motivators? Congratulations, whatever medium of expression you choose, on acknowledging such a thing as physical morality. There is no more explicable instance of an effort being its own reward.

Epilogue

Hail and farewell

Now it may be revealed that cross-training and triathlons are the first multisport systems not bound and shackled to preparing for war. The Olympic biathlon, consisting of cross-country skiing and sharpshooting, is a by-product of military training—being able to cover harsh terrain and suddenly drop to the ground and hit a target dead-on. Those ancient Greek pentathletes were warriors, and even swimming was once exclusively a soldier's skill. If there's ever a backlash against the "everyone's a winner" aspect of the cross-training movement, it can at least be argued that it has no plans to do anyone any harm.

On the contrary. The playfulness of it all provides something for everyone. I doubt I will ever again cover a story in which I am sent to Hawaii and, over the rum punch, be asked, "Were you at the carbo-load when Cowman started that food fight?" I don't like food fights and was glad I'd missed it, but I adored the alliteration. Because I understand things best by writing them down, I learned more about exuberance and fitness on this beat than I'd previously stored up in my lifetime. Someone once said that total fitness is really just a capacity for living. With that in mind, you'll

Rely on form toward the end of your run. Here Kurt Madden uses the crowd's enthusiasm to push himself to the finish line.

find that cross-training can become not only a system to accentuate endurance potential, but also a step into the sort of vitality that electrifies everything you touch.

Appendix

Magazines and newsletters that include Calendars of Events

Triathlon
  8461 Warner Drive
  Culver City, CA 90230
  (213) 558-3321
  or
  P.O. Box 5901
  Santa Monica, CA 90405
Running and Triathlon News
  5111 Santa Fe St.
  Suite 206
  San Diego, CA 92109
  (619) 270-4974
  Distributed in San Diego, Los Angeles,
  and Arizona
Tri-Fit
  575 Burns St.
  Penticton,
  British Columbia, V2A 1W9 Canada
  (604) 493-5181
  Quarterly
  Covering Canada and the Pacific Northwest
Tri-Athlete
  6660 Banning Dr.
  Oakland, CA 94611
  (415) 530-4580
The Complete Triathlete Newsletter
  P.O. Box 14842
  Chicago, IL 60014
  (312) 528-2893
  Will soon be replaced by
  Midwest Triathlete

The Beast
.   P.O. Box 643
     Wainscott, NY 11975
     (516) 324-1877
     Bimonthly tabloid

Triathlon Training Logs

Fleet Feet Press
     2410 J. St.
     Sacramento, CA 95816

Triathlon Training Equipment

Triathlete's Sportshop
     Box 5338
     Santa Monica, CA 90405
     Mail order—includes one of the few sources of tri-suits, triathlon T-
     shirts, training video cassettes, cold-water swimwear, etc.

Training Camps

Team Yosemite Triathlon Training Center
     Mark Doris
     P.O. Box 82
     Bass Lake, CA 93604
     (209) 642-3900
     Year-round consultation; train with Team Yosemite;
     individual programs designed
National Triathlon Training Camp
     1015 Gayley Ave.
     Suite 217
     Los Angeles, CA 90024
     (213) 466-9157
     Individual training during scheduled weekend
     sessions, films, lectures
New England Triathlon Camp
     Hank Lange
     33 Forest St.
     Brattleboro, VT 05301
     (802) 257-1208
Triathlon World
     P.O. Box 683
     Dennis, MA 02638
     Individual clinics (with videotaping), lectures

Camp Tri
    Ginny McConnell
    2410 J St.
    Sacramento, CA 95816
    (916) 442-8326 (days)
    Individual programs, run by top triathletes
Bob Curtis Triathlon Clinics
    4969 Central Dr. #207
    Stone Mountain, GA 30083
    (404) 469-7698

Clubs and Organizations

Southern California Triathlete's Club (SCTC)
    P.O. Box 10033
    Venice, CA 90291
    Sponsors a series of "tiny tri" races (½K swim, 20K bike, 5K run
    (about ¼, 12.5, 3 miles)
Bay Area Triathlon Club
    Box 5344
    San Francisco, CA 94101
    (415) 282-4491
Big Apple Tri Team
    Dan Honig
    301 E. 79th St. #30D
    New York, NY 10021
    (212) 288-5661
Hawaiian Bud Light Ironman World Championship
    (808) 528-2050
Tri-Fed/USA
    P.O. Box 2461
    Del Mar, CA 92014
    (619) 755-1663
    Provides insurance for sanctioned races; can refer members to
    events, clubs, or training camps in their area; $10 membership fee
Association of Professional Triathletes
    Bill Leach
    25108-B Marguerite Parkway #209
    Mission Viejo, CA 92692
    (714) 432-8826
    Organization for top professional triathletes
United States Triathlon Series
    P.O. Box 1438
    Davis, CA 95617
    (916) 758-9868
    City-to-city tour of triathlons; good distances for well-trained novices
    (1984 tour distances = 1.5K swim, 40K bike, 10K run)

7918